# ADVENTIST
# CULTURES IN CONFLICT

## Principles of Reconciliation

# A. Leroy Moore

Published by Moore Publishing
Print management by AB Publishing
Cover design by ChristianDsign.com
Illustrations by Honor Him Publishers
Editing by Kevin Morgan
Text design by Greg Solie • AltamontGraphics.com

Library of Congress Control Number:  2009902026

ISBN 978-160743-554-9

# —Contents—

# Memorial Letter to
## Simeon and Lettie Moore

It would be impossible to express the debt of appreciation I owe to Simeon and Lettie Moore. My mother and her father were baptized into the Seventh-day Adventist Church in 1908. My father with his mother and two brothers were baptized in 1912.

At barely seventeen years of age Mother left home permanently when her father, after reading D. M. Canright's *Adventism Renounced*, demanded that she attend meetings where he opposed the Church and especially Ellen White. She was

Lettie Moore (1896-1994)

thus on her own when she and my father wed in January 1917. A couple of years later they moved to California from the "sticks" of Idaho, where they had minimal contact with the Church and knew little about our lifestyle message. Daddy canvassed for a time in Oakland before they located at Paradise Valley where both enrolled in the nursing course. As their family began to grow they had to quit nurse's training, but continued their spiritual training as they faithfully attended all the regular and special services of the Church. They, and later we, were always grateful for the privilege they had to study under several who had been close associates of Ellen White. From them they absorbed many spiritual and practical principles.

Simeon Moore (1892-1959)

One of their mentors was Elder John Burden, the former manager of several sanitariums who had started the medical training that became Loma Linda University. Another mentor was Elder Luther Warren who, at fourteen years of age with another teenager named Harry Fenner, developed one of the first Seventh-day Adventist young people's societies. My parents were determined to teach the principles they learned from these men to their children. Their own teaching was simple, as their education was limited. Mother had less than a tenth grade education and Daddy never finished grade school, attending only a few months at a time, as he could be spared from farm duties. But there was depth and maturity to the principles they shared.

Mother's childhood dream was a dozen children to raise as workers for God. They didn't quite make the dozen, and three died in infancy. But they did raise eight of us. And all were actively engaged in church work. Due to loving and disciplined training, the six girls (four of whom were older than I) lived out the principles of true womanhood to my younger brother Paul and me. Their prayers and influence, along with those of our parents, held me during the years before I was personally converted.

My father had felt the call to the ministry but was unable to secure the education and was even forced by financial circumstances to drop out of nursing. Shortly before his death he expressed disappointment that he had accomplished so little in his life. I reminded him of the training he had given his children. Moreover, a small sampling of his lay ministry was evident at his unusually large funeral, where a number testified that he was instrumental in bringing them to the Lord.

My parents were among the early members of ASI, in which mother participated for four decades, mostly after my father went to his rest. Her ministry continued for thirty-five years after his passing. During that time she continued their ministry to what she affectionately called, "my elderlies," many younger than she. During those years over a hundred young people called her "mother." These she boarded while they were in college or provided them a haven or helped them overcome alcohol or drug addiction. Some of these became workers in the Adventist cause, including evangelist, Dan Collins, whose only training in ministry came from her.

While in her late 80s and early 90s, Mother traveled with me in my Native work, serving as my receptionist and visiting homes with me. I shall always remember the love she shared and which was returned from the Native people. Her love of beauty and inspiration at seeing the beauties as we traveled was an inspiration to me, and so was her eagerness to learn, which lasted ninety eight years.

My parents' heritage was their children, whom they ever kept before the Lord. Myrtle, my oldest sister, was a church school teacher and active church worker. Miriam is still active in church work at 85. At the time of Daddy's death, she had taught nursing for thirteen years in Ethiopia and would teach nursing at Pacific Union College until retirement. Milli had served as a lab technician, but was then working with mother at her "Rose Haven" ministry for the elderly. Marie, mother's mainstay for years, had with her husband begun more than forty years as Pathfinder leaders (at 88, his Pathfindering has now covered over half a century).

Marilyn was married and active in her church at that time, but would soon return home to work with my mother at Rose Haven. As mother grew older they exchanged places; Marilyn became manager and mother her helper. She, with her husband Charles Sterling, would manage it until her death. Theirs was not an institution, but a home where each guest was treated as family. Together with Peter, whom Marilyn and my mother trained years ago, Charles is still continuing the loving tradition. Three of the five girls are now sleeping in Jesus, awaiting the call of the Lifegiver.

Marcia, my youngest sister, was still in her teens when Daddy died. But she even then was interested in children and dedicated her life to teaching the cradle roll/kindergarten tots. As did her sisters, she also helped mother for several years. I had been in the ministry a few years when Daddy died and Paul returned from the seminary to be with him during his last months. Since then, he and I both pastored and taught college until retirement. He completed his ministry by developing "Life Talk Radio." And I was privileged to pioneer as the General Conference/NAD Native American Ministries Coordinator.

I speak for us all, including the three who now sleep in Jesus and would heartily join my testimony—what a great blessing we received from parents who were dedicated not merely to the Church, but to Christ, and who treasured His Word and held fast His testimonies!

Left to right front: Milli (3), Marie (4), Mother (Lettie), Marilyn (7), Myrtle (1)
Left to right back: Leroy (5), Miriam (2), Marcia (8), Paul (6)

# —Appreciation—

My greatest appreciation goes to my wonderful wife of nearly fifty-seven years for her continued support and proofreading of my writing. I also thank Weimar College administrators for the opportunity to write without the burden of classes.

So many have helped me in preparing this book that I fear leaving important ones out. Yet, I do want to honor their enthusiastic interest and help.

Among those who have offered suggestions and encouragement are seven Australians: Eric and Carol Livingston, Glyn Parfitt, Scott Charlesworth, John Raynor, Randall Ibbitt, and Jan Knopper. What a wonder email is, to make those across the world as accessible as next door neighbors!

Others include: Richard Davidson, Paul Giem, Jack Blanco, Herbert Douglass, Jerry Moon, Larry Evans, Woody Whidden, Bryce Pasco, David Conklin, Hubert Sturges, Gary Warner, Alvin Fisher, Andy Anderson, Inge Anderson, Robert Wolfgramm, John and Sharon Witcombe, David and Laura Schwimmer, and, last but by no means least, Mary Morris, whose enthusiasm is a joy.

Special thanks go to Doctors Richard and Lorna Lukens for providing the means to publish this book. I am also indebted to Kevin Morgan, of whom I knew nothing, but to whom David Conklin gave a copy of the manuscript. Convinced of its importance, he set aside his other work to provide a detailed critique that helped shape the final form of the chapters. I also want to express special appreciation to Jerry Moon, who felt he could not take time to write a Foreword, but who was impressed to set aside his other work to do it.

To all these I express deep gratitude, not only for their suggestions and encouragement, but especially for the sense of mutual ownership of principles as we sought to present them clearly.

My praise, however, is to the Lord for His guidance. It seems providential that I wrote chapters nearly two decades ago as part of the *Adventism in Conflict* manuscript that became the basis for this book. Considering the manuscript vital, but too large for best impact, fifteen years ago Woody Whidden offered to help me reduce its size. For years I virtually forgot that the chapters relating to culture were waiting to be formed into a new book. I have since adapted and expanded them. I am convinced that the issues are more pertinent now than they were in 1994. (At the request of many, I hope soon to republish *Adventism in Conflict*, which provides a more detailed examination of the principles in this book.)

# —Foreword—

For more than 50 years, Leroy Moore has been wrestling with the philosophical issues that have now grown into a culture war within Adventism. As a young pastor in 1956, he was already grappling with the issue of the humanity of Christ in relation to the humanity of sinners. This led to an MA thesis in 1966 on "Ellen G. White's Concept of the Nature of Man as It Relates to the Objectives of Bible Teaching." His first published book on these issues was *Theology in Crisis* (1979), a New York University Ph.D. dissertation comparing Ellen G. White's concept of righteousness by faith with the "Reformationist theology" of Desmond Ford. In 1995, the Review and Herald published his *Adventism in Conflict*, a book I used as a supporting textbook for seminary courses in the Development of Seventh-day Adventist Theology until the book went out of print. Moore used the same principles to elucidate a different aspect of the problem in *Questions on Doctrine Revisited* (2005). Thus the present book, *Adventist Cultures in Conflict*, represents the matured fruit of Moore's long reflection on the causes of the "conservative" vs. "liberal" divide in Adventism.

His own varied experience has prepared him to critique the multi-sided issues of *Adventist Cultures in Conflict*. He has served in denominational employment as a pastor in the Alaska, Southern New England, Texico, and Upper Columbia conferences; as a Bible teacher at Solusi, Walla Walla, and Columbia Union Colleges; and as Coordinator of Native American Work for the North American Division. He has also served in parachurch entities as director of La Vida Mission (New Mexico), president of Lavoy Missionary College (Alberta), and Bible teacher at Weimar College.

Moore's published contribution is both developmental and cumulative. Persons with a serious commitment to resolving the issues that divide us may want to read all four of his published books in sequence. The principles that he uncovers become clearer as he applies them to different historical events and theological issues in the Adventist experience.

In some ways, *Adventist Cultures in Conflict* is the most philosophically foundational of Moore's works. He defines and uses the term 'paradoxical' to describe aspects of truth that are *apparently*, but not actually, in conflict. In direct contrast to 'paradoxical,' he uses 'dialectical' to describe the intellectual process by which polar aspects of truth are artificially separated, so that a whole truth is fractured into competing 'split-truths,' distortions which taken separately do not constitute the whole truth. Moore traces the problem of truth-splitting back to Plato, who employed his dialectic in a deliberate attempt to undermine the lifework of his mentor Socrates.

Moore's concept of "poles" of truth to be held in unity is similar to the "elliptical principle" of Herbert Douglass, who uses the two foci of an ellipse to represent aspects of knowledge that together constitute a unified truth. Douglass declares that "Truth is radically altered when one focus of the ellipse of truth is overemphasized at the expense of the other." Douglass, *Messenger of the Lord* (Pacific Press, 1998), p. 266, note 47; cf. pp. 260–263, 573–575.

Moore shows how human self-centeredness and nearsightedness predispose each of us to focus on the pole of truth most congenial to our personal temperament, lifestyle, or cultural context—leading us to diminish the opposite pole that is really an essential element of the same truth. An example of a united and a split truth would be the full deity and full humanity of Jesus Christ. Overemphasizing His deity at the expense of His humanity leads to the heresy of docetism which does not see Christ's body as genuinely human. Overemphasizing His humanity at the expense of His deity leads to the heresy of adoptionism which sees Him as a great man, but not as Incarnate God. Split-truths, emphasized over or separated from their complementary aspects, develop opposing dialects that can barely understand each other and eventually become systemically divergent cultures.

Moore finds both strengths and weaknesses in both conservative and progressive viewpoints. What perpetuates the cultural divide is the human tendency of all to see their own strengths and others' faults, while overlooking their own faults and others' strengths. Moore urges that the solution must begin with individuals on both sides focusing on Jesus, humbly acknowledging their faults, and seeking His power to crucify pride and relate in humility to those they differ from—without anyone on either side compromising conscience.

When proponents of each side honor those they differ with and seek to put the best possible construction on their word, acts, and motives, each will be enabled to recognize the genuine truth held by those with whom they differ. As aspects of truth held by one culture are united with aspects of truth held by the other culture, the combination will more closely approximate the "whole" truth. In light of this more complete grasp of truth, both sides will be better enabled to discern and renounce the defects in their own perceptions of truth.

Moore climaxes his argument by analyzing in detail how progressives and conservatives, though seemingly blind to their own faults, each see clearly the other's faults. If each would humble themselves to respectfully listen to and learn from the other, conservatives and progressives could both truly serve each other as friendly critics, and correct each other's faults. Otherwise, we not only perpetuate the conflict, but in the process, each side tends to neutralize the positive contribution of the other.

Throughout the book, Moore argues repeatedly that this cultural divide is an intellectual and spiritual conflict which cannot be solved by intellect alone. All participants need the Holy Spirit to cure their spiritual blindness and to aid them in working out these principles in experience. Until the principles are both understood and worked out in experience, the Adventist culture wars will continue.

A strong sense of urgency resonates in the book, because what began as a theological disagreement in the 1950s has now matured into sharply diverging cultures within Adventism. How much wider can the chasm grow without actual schism?

The cosmic controversy is not between progressives and conservatives. Persons from both sides will be saved, and persons from both sides will be lost. The conflict between selfishness and truth runs right through every mind and heart, and only as Adventists on both sides die to self can they see clearly their own flaws or recognize truth in someone who speaks a different theological dialect or conforms to a different religious culture.

Jerry Moon
Associate Professor of Church History
Seventh-day Adventist Theological Seminary
Andrews University

# —Introduction—

Some Seventh-day Adventists today encourage theological pluralism which invites a variety of doctrinal positions and in which membership is determined not by core beliefs but by cultural identity. Those who favor this form of pluralism welcome it as the wave of the future. But it is viewed with grave concern by those who believe Seventh-day Adventism is not merely a church. They consider it a movement divinely called to proclaim God's last-day message to worship the Creator and to escape the confusion of the religious system known as Babylon, a system which embraces all religious and even non-religious beliefs.

The purpose of this book is to demonstrate that our movement is endangered by both conservative and liberal cultures. Thus, not one but two competing cultures threaten the integrity of God's last-day message and our mission to proclaim it in purity. Each culture emphasizes one of two balancing poles of truth: law and obedience or grace and faith. Neither of these can itself fulfil our commission; for neither alone properly represents our message. Indeed, when separated each poses a threat to both message and mission.

## Competing Cultures Develop Competing Languages

These competing cultures have developed competing languages. They have much the same vocabulary; but there are marked differences in the way that vocabulary is interpreted, indicated by frequency and context of use as well as emphasis and intonation. Moreover, each language is very offensive to the other. Unfortunately, the more intensely that each culture reacts to the other, the greater will be the shift for both from the center and the unity of truth. That I deal primarily with these opposite parties does not suggest that all identify with one party or the other. By no means are all involved directly or even consciously in conflict; yet, the principles I discuss are vital to all of us.

The chapters in this book were adapted from materials excised from the *Adventism in Conflict* manuscript, which was published by *Review* in 1995. In it I tell of my youthful discovery that truth is by nature paradoxical; that is, it always contains balancing principles. The original manuscript introduced 'dialectical' as an antonym of 'paradoxical.' But as the book became too long I cut out 60% of the book's contents, including these chapters which relate to dialectical (or 'split-truth') thinking that underlies the confusion of mystical Babylon (Rev. 14:8, 18) and its conflicting cultures and competing 'languages.' It would thus be well to read this book in relation to *Adventism in Conflict*.

## What God Hath Joined Together, Let No Man Put Asunder

By 'paradoxical' I never refer either to contradiction or to compromise of truth, but always to the balancing principles of Bible truth themselves. Although each pole is absolutely essential to the integrity of the other pole of truth, they often appear to contradict one another and are thus frequently pitted against each other by defenders of one against the other.

Since 'paradoxical' and 'dialectical' are key terms throughout this book, I will at the outset more specifically state my working definitions—definitions to which you may want to refer later on.

**Paradoxical**: Unfortunately, this term is used in different and even opposite ways. But by paradoxical I always refer to that which appears contradictory, yet in reality is not. Paradoxical thus refers to truth that seems to involve contradictory ideas. To be completely true, however, both ideas must be held together in tension, and thus in balance.[1] Note the overt paradox in opposite statements of consecutive verses in Proverbs; they seem to contradict each other, but both are essential in knowing how to deal with a fool:

| | |
|---|---|
| *Answer not a fool according to his folly, lest thou also be like unto him.* | *Answer a fool according to his folly, lest he be wise in his own conceit.* |
| *—Proverbs 26:4.* | *—Proverbs 26:5.* |

The former warns against lowering oneself to the level of a fool by arguing with him; the latter identifies the fool's need to be challenged. Unlike this example, most paradoxes are neither contradictory in statement nor so obvious.

**Dialectical**: This term is also used in very different and converse ways. But its method, which pits opposite poles against each other, destroys paradoxical principles. To follow my use of the term, it is essential to clearly grasp this contrast. Instead of uniting converse principles of truth, as does paradoxical thinking, dialectical thinking separates them. By a "Socratic" process of reasoning, it does finally bring them together, but never as a balanced whole. Instead, the product is a third position that distorts both principles.

Thus, by 'dialectical,' I always refer to splitting the sphere of truth into opposite hemispheres, so that, instead of complementing or completing each other, the principles are set against one another. A 'dialectical' focus on one pole subordinates

---

1   Concerning opposite uses of 'paradoxical,' Hastings' *Encyclopaedia of Religion and Ethics* defines paradox as "both real and only apparent contradiction." Significantly, however, it concludes: "*Truth* may be—perhaps even in the end *must be*—***paradoxical***" (vol. ix, p. 632, emphasis added). This confirms the basic meaning of paradoxical as dipolar truth in which each of two converse principles is essential ("must be") to the integrity of the other. (More on the different uses of this term in Appendix A.)

the balancing principle; thus, neither pole is permitted either to balance or to be balanced by the other.

By contrast, paradoxical thinking never pits one pole of truth against the other and never seeks to demonstrate the superiority of one principle over the other. It acknowledges tension in all truth, but protects both poles and seeks to grasp their inner harmony so as to fully uphold and demonstrate the necessity of each to the other. Rather than subordinating one principle to the other, let us learn to honor the principles of unity involved in both poles of truth. As the preacher in the wedding ceremony declares: "What therefore God hath joined together, let not man put asunder" (cf. Matt. 19:6).

## *Dialectical* Thinking Imposes Compromise; *Paradoxical* Thinking Prevents It

Dialectical processes repeatedly synthesize truth's poles, but never truly unite them in a way to retain the integrity of their balancing principles. Dialectical synthesis always involves compromise, with one pole of truth subordinating or taking the other up into itself and thus controlling its meaning so that each loses its capacity to balance the other. This process not only causes serious conflicts and misunderstandings that divide Adventism, but, as we shall see, now threatens the very stability of civilization.

Paradoxical principles, on the other hand, prevent compromise by requiring the poles of truth to be kept in tension so that neither can control the other. As both are thus retained in full strength they not only support each other, but each sets divinely ordained parameters for the other. In dialectical processes, one is always compromised by control of the other. Indeed, the function and meaning of both are compromised; for unless each provides the proper context and balance for the other, neither can function according to its divine purpose.

## Law vs. Grace: Pitting Truth Against Truth

The most common and serious result of dialectical reasoning is the pitting of law and grace against each other, with each side of the argument seeking to control the meaning of the one it considers to be secondary. However, neither principle can be understood except in relation to the fullness of the other. When the principle of law dominates the principle of grace, the result is legalism. Grace is not usually denied; but is subordinated to law so that it can no longer set the parameters of law. By contrast, when grace subordinates law, the result is antinomianism which resists and even opposes law; for law can no longer speak for itself or establish the nature of grace. This is serious, for grace is only truly appreciated when law is understood.

Our conflicts are perpetuated by dialectical 'split-truth' languages which place truth in conflict with truth. To participate in the final proclamation of our message in 'loud cry' power we must first escape the cultural languages we unwittingly borrow from antitypical Babylon, symbolized by its confusion of conflicting tongues (Gen. 11). We must break free from the contrary, conceptual languages and cultures by which Satan enslaves mystical Babylon (Rev. 18:1–4).

To shift our focus from law and obedience to Christ crucified, God sent us the "Minneapolis message." E. J. Waggoner and A. T. Jones powerfully proclaimed a Christ-centered message that unites and preserves intact both poles of truth. Sadly, *split-truth* thinking stimulated a strong reaction by key leaders against their message that precipitated the 1888 conflict. Sadder still, Waggoner and Jones later split the poles of truth in other ways and fell away through intense theological and administrative conflict. In his intense focus on individualism, Jones became so imbalanced as to declare the Adventist Church Babylon for its organization!

## Organization of this Book

Part One of this book treats cultural issues in relation to ancient and modern society. Special focus is given to mystical Babylon and the underlying factors involved in the world's wars faced since the 1798 unsealing of Daniel's prophecies. Chapter 1 tells how two experiences set the direction of my ministry; Chapters 2 to 4 portray my problem with a doctoral professor that led to my selection of the term 'dialectical' as an antonym of 'paradoxical.' The remaining chapters of Part One deal with the cultural and political conflicts resulting from 'dialectical' thinking which not only create conflict within Adventism but threatens society.

Part Two develops these principles in relation to our Adventist conflicts and in the context of the straight testimony of the Laodicean message. Its purpose is to prepare us to give the three angels' messages in Latter Rain power. Moreover, the key to this power is found in the Minneapolis call to focus upon and proclaim Christ and His righteousness.

After exploring our two cultures—one based on law; the other on grace—and principles relating to our conflict over celebration worship, I will conclude Part Two with chapters that deal with the judgment and the straight testimony of the Laodicean message. When the message Waggoner and Jones once powerfully proclaimed removes our split-languages, we will proclaim our message in a language of truth that will unite its polar principles into a single focus on Christ, the embodiment of grace and whose character is a transcript of the law.

# Part 1
## Dialectical Cultures and Conflicting Languages

—Chapter 1—
## Integrity Requires Honest Testing

*"Quench not the Spirit. ... Prove all things; hold fast that which is good."*
*—1 Thessalonians 5:19–21.*

In my youth I felt indignant at the blind dogmatism of Jehovah's Witnesses. Those I came in contact with demanded to be heard, but refused to listen! They sought to control the discussion by repeating memorized questions and jumping quickly to another topic when faced with a question they could not answer. Programmed to impose their view of Scripture, they refused to allow the Bible to speak for itself.

As a result of such encounters, I began to question myself: *Am I not also certain I am right and far more interested in speaking than in listening?* With a sense of calling to the ministry from my earliest memories, I eagerly looked forward to engaging in evangelism. My concern about not following Jehovah's Witness patterns came to a head near the close of my first year in college. Having been guided by teachers and by prepared materials in my Bible study, I felt I must now face the challenges of opponents by Scripture alone and with the same openness I expected of others. Only in this way could I be sure of dealing fairly with opponents and honestly with truth.

Yet, I became anxious when the security of dogmatic faith was set aside to test my doctrinal view with no commitment except to the Bible. Nonetheless, the die was cast. The integrity of my ministry—yes, even of my very life—was at stake.

The Mormon subjection of belief in Scripture to the authority of Joseph Smith and the ongoing line of Mormon prophets posed a specific challenge to my thinking. I knew that if they were to test Mormonism by the Bible, their view of truth would be very different. I did not doubt the prophetic role of Ellen White. But I could not ask Mormons to test their prophets by Scripture unless I would seriously perform the same test on Ellen White's prophetic gift and on our doctrines. Such a test would require that I do more than seek evidence to prove them. I must truly test each one, just as I expected them to do.

## Facing the Fear of What I Might Find

What if I found conflict between Ellen White and the Bible? The answer was clear. If her messages were from Christ, I need not fear. Yet I did fear. I feared being led into false paths by the deceiver of a third of heaven's angels—the one whose agents destroyed the faith of my own grandfather three years after his 1908 baptism and who spent the rest of his life fighting Ellen White and the Seventh-day Adventist Church. I feared that my own pride and independence might betray me.

That kind of fear is not only warranted but vital. Indeed, it is essential to the development of unwavering faith. Had Grandpa Wheeler only re-examined our doctrines with faith in God and distrust of self he would not have gone astray. Fear of one's own pride is prerequisite to the growth of faith in God's grace. As Eve's encounter at the tree of knowledge teaches, independence-based pride engenders unbelief. Thus, our hope lies in a healthy, non-neurotic, distrust of self.

As I tested each of our pillar doctrines with earnest intercession that I not be permitted to stray, my confidence in our message greatly increased. I found that wrestling with apparent contradictions in Scripture provided the most vital insights into truth.

## Challenge of Jehovah's Witness Sets Direction of My Ministry

Five years later, as a young pastor in Fairbanks, Alaska, I faced a different challenge from a Jehovah's Witness leader who was well versed in both the Bible and Adventist doctrine. Moreover, he was armed with a fist full of perplexing Ellen  White quotations. By a process of questions, he put these quotations and Bible passages in a light very different from what I had seen before, as he argued that "Christ was totally and only a man." I responded with evidences of His divinity, but was not myself satisfied with the answers I gave him.

That night I determined to re-examine that issue from Scripture alone. Thus, once more, asking God to protect me against deception, I searched for many weeks every Bible passage that in any way related to the subject. Truth bears investigation. Thus, my confidence in our message and in the Spirit of prophecy only increased. Indeed, the principles that brought unity to Scriptural passages also brought unity to the statements of Ellen White that were questioned.[2]

---

2    Jehovah's Witnesses have high moral standards and hold many vital truths. However, their focus on a single pole of truth forces that truth to serve error. Zealous to defend Christ's human nature, they repudiate the balancing truth of His divinity. Thus they divide truth into two conceptual languages and deny one principle to defend the other.

Once again I found in apparent contradictions special avenues for deepening insights into truth. In fact, by the time I finished, I had concluded that *truth is itself paradoxical*. From an external or superficial standpoint there may appear to be contradiction; but the apparently contradictory principles are so internally essential to each other that neither pole of truth can be truly understood except in relation to the other.

## One-Pole Focus on Truth Breeds Opposite Heresies

I had come in contact with Liberals who downplayed what I knew to be truth, but I soon saw that Liberals are not alone in splitting truth and focusing upon one principle at the expense of the other. Conservatives unwittingly do the same, but in opposite ways. Whereas Liberals subordinate law to grace; Conservatives tend to subordinate grace to law. Unless we depend on the Holy Spirit's guidance, we inevitably subordinate one principle to the other, and are left with knowledge void of true understanding.

I had no idea when I confirmed the divine nature of Christ in far off Fairbanks, Alaska in 1956 that the publication of *Questions on Doctrine*, a year later, would ignite conflict within Adventism over Christ's human nature.

The issue for Adventists was not whether He was human, but whether He took Adam's sinless nature before the fall or his sinful nature after the fall. I praised God, when that conflict arose, for the paradoxical keys He gave me to clarify the issues.

---

The more vital the truth, the more important it is to carefully examine and preserve its balancing principles.

—Chapter 2—

# Resigning My Goals to God's Opening Providence

*"Commit thy way unto the* LORD; *trust also in him, and he shall bring it to pass." —Psalm 37:5.*

Two decades after my research and the *Questions on Doctrine* explosion, I looked forward to a fourteen-month, salary-and-expenses-paid study leave from Columbia Union College to do my doctoral dissertation and probe issues in continuous conflict because of our failure to grasp both sides of key Bible paradoxes. However, in the hardest decision of my life I, instead, resigned my position to direct La Vida, a deeply indebted Navajo mission with staff tensions so high that all the teachers and deans had turned in their resignations as of the close of the school year.

The finances and staff problems were not my main concern. I was reluctant to leave college teaching and knew that I might never complete my doctorate. With neither the savings to finance it myself, nor the prospect of being able to save in a lay-funded ministry, it seemed likely that my allotted time for finishing the dissertation would run out.

Having repeatedly turned down the call to La Vida, I again declined when Dr. Erl Hendrickson, a boyhood friend who was then vice chairman of the board, called to urge me to accept. However, I did agree to pray about it. And, as I prayed, the conviction began to grow that this was an answer to my prayer.

Because our son had dyslexia and needed to escape the competitive pressure of school, I had told the Lord that, if necessary, I would leave denominational work and get a job that would allow me to work with David. Recognizing in this call an answer to my prayer, I resigned and moved to La Vida.

## That Decision Proved Essential to My Doctoral Dissertation

When Desmond Ford suddenly appeared on my theological horizon immediately after I made that decision, I sensed that a divine purpose for this detour involved more than my son. I was not ready to begin my dissertation. Ford's issues were directly related to the ones I intended to probe; yet it would take time to ponder his new questions and to secure materials for use in my dissertation. In fact, Ford had not yet written many of the documents detailing his views that I would need. Moreover, he was still in Australia, and it would have been almost impossible to have the friendly personal interchanges between us that proved so vital in preparing me to write.

## Seeing Through Ford's Lenses

Three years later, Ford was teaching at Pacific Union College when my sister Milli and her husband, Richard Westmoreland, invited us to stay in their basement apartment at Angwin, where I could be in personal touch with Ford as I examined his views in my dissertation.

As I sought to penetrate his perspectives, a sense of joy often stirred within me as truths over which we wrestled grew sharper and more impressive. I was amazed at how identical the pieces of our views were, yet how differently we put those pieces together. At almost any point of difference on the highway of truth, we would identify the same issues and share similar convictions—only to drive away in opposite directions.

It appeared to me that Ford habitually violated paradoxical principles by splitting truth into separate hemispheres and magnifying one at the expense of the other. Yet the question haunted me: *Could I be the one with a blind eye?* As I scrutinized his view for any overlooked key and carefully questioned him to make sure I fully understood his position, I prayerfully re-examined my own patterns of thought to assure faithfulness to paradoxical principles.

When Ford enthusiastically affirmed every element in the second chapter of my dissertation, which outlines his concepts, I was certain I did not misunderstand his position and was convinced that he did indeed consistently rupture paradoxical unity on the issues involved.

## Splitting Truth's Sphere Makes Two Opposing Hemispheres

Endless conflict within Christendom from the Apostles' day to ours testifies to a universal bent toward dialectic thinking which cuts *through* (*dia*) truth and makes *two* contrasting theological *languages* (*lectic*). To cut through the diameter of a circle makes two opposite halves out of the whole. The same thing happens when the sphere of truth is divided. It creates two opposite, part-truth hemispheres. Yet both parts are required to make a whole. The language derived from half of the truth does convey vital part-truth, but each part-truth is isolated and insulated from its converse complement of truth.

The speaker of each language instinctively resists or opposes the opposite part-truth, so that the incomplete parts cannot unite in a single whole. In such dividing of the poles of truth, rarely is either denied; instead, each adherent of a part-truth seeks to subordinate the other part-truth to the one he or she defends.

Regardless which pole is defended, subordination of the other violates truth and undermines the authority of God's Word. The more intense the subordination, the more serious is the violation. Moreover, the degree of distinction in language depends on the degree of emphasis placed upon one pole over the other. There are thus not just two languages—liberal and conservative. Both languages have many "dialects," each of which violates the paradoxical language of truth.

## What the Poles of Truth Look Like

The two poles of truth can be identified in many pairs. An important pair of poles is subjective and objective. Others which relate to these include invisible vs. visible, abstract vs. concrete, and internal vs. external, etc. Generally the first pole relates to or involves divine attributes, gifts, or activities (i.e., grace and the gift of faith); while the second pole relates to human response (such as obedience to law). Indeed, the most debated pair throughout history is grace (received internally) and law (obeyed literally).

The divine-human nature of truth is most clearly seen in respect to divine revelation. One pole of revelation is divine communication, the other is human expression of that communication. The paradoxical issue involves determining and honoring the aspects that reveal eternal divine truth as well as those that reflect human culture. Indeed, whatever specific balancing factors are in focus, the parts tend to relate in some way to divine and human elements of truth.[3]

But these various elements may be seen in different ways. For example, we generally see law and grace as converse poles (human obedience to law and divine grace). Yet, the law is itself divine, just as is grace; and faith which leads to obedience, is a divine gift. In this light, law and grace are not opposite poles, but aspects of the same divine pole. The paradoxical opposites in this context are *human exercise of the divine gift of faith* and *human obedience to divine law*.

---

3    It is highly significant that Herbert Douglass and I developed two different paradigms to explain the same principles. Neither of us knew of the others work for many years. I was delighted, in the '80s, to hear Herb present, by his ellipsis, principles that I, for three decades, had expressed in paradoxical terms. In his kind critique of the manuscript for this book, he attached a copy of his November 22, 2008, Adventist Theological Society address. Since it clearly explains and demonstrates the parallel principles of his ellipsis, I include an abbreviation of it in this book as Appendix B. Those acquainted with his excellent paradigm may at first want to translate my 'paradox' by "ellipsis."

In whatever perspective, to subordinate either pole to the other is to alter the meaning of both. Balance requires that each pole set parameters for understanding the other. Thus, when either controls the other, balance is destroyed and both principles are subverted.

A major cause of conflict in Christianity for millennia—and the primary cause of conflict within Adventism—has been the subordination of divine grace to human obedience, or the subordination of human obedience to superficial concepts of divine grace. The latter produces an antinomian culture and its language of grace, with its resistance to law, while the former produces a legalistic culture and its language of law.

## Home and Social Group Determine the Infant's Language

Culture always begins first and produces a corresponding language that expresses that culture. A baby is born into a home culture and begins to absorb that culture before he or she is able to talk. Being born in a spiritually mature home, however, does not mean that the child will grow up speaking a balanced language of truth.

Unless a child is born again, it can only develop carnally—no matter how balanced the religious culture in which he or she grows up. Moreover, the greater the effort of an unconverted child to follow the example of spiritual parents, the more intense will be the development of a language of law. Only by the presence and direction of the Spirit can grace and law unite in experience.

## Paradox Never Refers to Facts, but to Principles* of Truth

Since both culture/languages are imbalanced, neither is truly satisfying. Those who sense a consequent emptiness of soul and feel defeated face three choices: (a) remain empty and defeated and possibly give up and leave the church; (b) switch languages, either convert from Liberal to Conservative or, more likely, going with the flow, convert from Conservative to Liberal; or (c) be born again by the Spirit into a heavenly culture of unselfish love and learn to speak the balanced language of truth. Unless or until we do experience the new birth, we will not think paradoxically and we can only remain slaves to one culture and its language or to the other.

Before proceeding, I need to mention that facts, such as the fact of a literal six-day creation, are not paradoxical. Facts do not need balancing. Indeed, they cannot be "balanced" by something else. Any attempt to balance facts only distorts them. Bible facts only need to be honored as divinely-revealed realities. But while the six days and consecration of the seventh are only historical facts, our relation

---

* Webster defines a "principle" as "a comprehensive and fundamental law, doctrine, or assumption" and also as "a rule or code of conduct."

to these is paradoxical. Emphasizing the six literal days of creation and obeying the Sabbath command, outside the context of loving communion with our Creator, produces legalism.

Similarly, paradoxical thinking does not mean the merging of theories of truth. Any attempt to arrive at truth by merging human theories is worse than useless. Only Bible principles need integrating. Moreover, balance does not mean always giving equal emphasis to each pole of truth. The inviolable rule is that we never uphold one principle by undermining or minimizing its converse and complementary principle.

## Waggoner and Jones First Restored the Poles of Truth, Then They Split Them Apart

Why has the paradoxical vs. dialectical issue become so important to us? The message given to our early Adventist pioneers focused sharply upon obedience to God's law in the context of a judgment determined by that law. By itself, this would produce an imbalanced focus upon law and obedience, but the vital context for the judgment was our sanctuary message, which portrays Christ as our High Priest, the Author of the law and the source of grace. As long as our focus was upon Him, the result was a balanced language of truth. *For He unites the poles of truth in Himself.*

Unfortunately, in reaction to the language of grace used by opponents who had repudiated the law, we unwittingly shifted our primary focus from Christ to His law and began to view any emphasis on grace as a subtle undermining of God's law.

To call our people back to the balance of truth essential to the 'loud cry'[4] of the Latter Rain, God gave E. J. Waggoner and A. T. Jones a message to correct our language of law. But their focus on Christ, who is the Source of all truth and in whom alone we find the balance of truth, met intense opposition. Key leaders identified their message with evangelical antinomianism. They were sure the young preachers were calling for the first step in repudiating the law and its Sabbath.

E. J. Waggoner

Sadly, in the long controversy that followed, both men lost their own focus on Christ and thereby lost the integrated power of the message that restored a balanced language of

Alonzo T. Jones

---

4    The 'loud cry' is a term given Ellen White to describe the repetition of the third angel's message in Rev. 18:1–3. In RH 12-31-1857, she uses it in connection with the 'latter rain' end-time refreshing from the presence of the Lord.

truth. Satan, whose master strategy is to impose dialectical (*split-language*) conflict, thus caused both parties to lose their focus upon Christ in imbalanced attempts to correct the imbalance of the other. The sad result was that Waggoner and Jones ended up splitting the very language of truth they were sent to restore.

It is now our task to restore a pure language of integrated truth which alone can remove the dialectical 'split-truth' conflict Satan induces. But the experience of Waggoner and Jones warns us that no one is secure—even when proclaiming balanced truth, as they did,—unless the focus remains upon the Source of truth, the only One who can unite its converse principles.

# —Chapter 3—
# A Rejection That Leads to a Solution

*"The fear of the* Lord *is the beginning of knowledge." —Proverbs 1:7.*

I now invite you to go with me to a New York University class to introduce a textbook that would later help get me off the hook when my professor refused my papers for his class. The name of the textbook is *Two Logics: The Conflict Between Classical and Neo-analytic Philosophy.* That refusal led me to adopt the term, 'dialectical' as an antonym for 'paradoxical.'

The author of the book, Henry B. Veatch, warns of two logics (similar to the "two languages") employed in scientific endeavor. One is based on objective science and the other on subjective scientific philosophy. The latter appears to be objective because it relates to "facts" and/or "statistics," but its philosophical deductions so impose culturally-accepted norms upon scientific findings that the facts do not and cannot speak for themselves. That is, the assumptions it brings to the investigation of objective data involve a worldview pre-set by educational and societal conditioning that determine how the facts themselves are perceived. The product is thus not objective, but subjective.

The name, Sir Karl Popper, renowned philosopher-scientist, occurred frequently in *Two Logics* and was often on my professor's lips. That name would suggest a key to the problem I would face when the professor rejected my papers and forced me to do vastly more study than should have been required. Ironically, it was this refusal of my papers that also led me to the handle I needed to identify the opposite of paradoxical thinking.

## A Most Unusual Professor

The crisis began when Dr. Parkinson, professor in my last NYU doctoral class History of Education, refused to accept the papers I wrote in fulfilment of his assignments. Since there were no tests and no other assignments, those papers constituted the sole basis for my grade!

Parkinson was the most unusual teacher I ever knew. We were to read six texts on education, for which he had prepared critiques specifically challenging the evolutionary theory of each author. We were then to critique any four of his critiques and turn them in at any time during the term. Most unusual was his demand that we *not* agree with him, but challenge his position, and we would not know the results until the term grades were later mailed out.

I had never known a professor who so insistently demanded that students challenge his concepts. Indeed, he graciously accepted challenges, even by two communists in the class, despite how contrary their concepts were to his key principle of freedom. Freedom to him meant freedom from law. Indeed, one of the six texts was about an elementary-high school with no rules at all, except that there be no rules. Every student was to act upon his own impulses freely and without restraint, including sexual impulses in a co-ed school with no separate dorms.

Wanting to give primary attention to my dissertation proposal class in which I would write my first chapter, I decided to do all four papers as quickly as possible and then give full attention to the proposal and start my dissertation. With classes only one day a week, I worked night and day on his class, reading all six texts and doing the critiques. This meant challenging his Darwinian theory four times, since each of his critiques defended his Darwinian concept of freedom against the particular evolutionary theory of that author.

I could easily affirm freedom. God prizes freedom so highly that He risked His own life to give man free choice and then died to restore and guarantee that freedom. However, challenging Parkinson on the nature of freedom would hit him in the solar plexus—four times! He strongly reacted against the very idea of a Creator, for this introduces law, design, and authority. And this, he insisted, robs us of freedom.

In his system, children must never be taught what truth is; for there is no such thing. There is only being. They must only be taught to think for themselves and learn from their own experience. Parkinson failed to see that with no principles that govern experience, children could not even evaluate their experience and could only become unwitting slaves to whatever culture surrounded them.

## Blind Surrender to the Darwinian Lie of No Objective Truth

How could an educated man take such an extreme position as to pit the need for experience against the need to understand principles that govern experience? How could one be more bound by his own dialectical, 'split-truth' view? Only because he totally "surrendered" to the lie that there is no objective truth; there is only an evolving process. Thus, no one has any right to interfere with the "natural" development of any other, no matter how young. To him the height of evil was to interfere with the absolute freedom of another, even in the education process, for, with no objective laws, all development is by evolutionary chance. Thus, young or old, each human being becomes a law unto himself.

How could I retain integrity and write papers that would satisfy his "no law" exclusion of a Creator? My one comfort was that he had treated the communist students with respect—even though the entire system of communism rejects the principle of freedom. As I set about to establish that true freedom requires law, I only hoped he would be as lenient to my challenging of his freedom principle as he was to the communists.

Without reference to God or to Scripture, I illustrated the principle of freedom by natural law. Pole-vaulters and runners, for example, study carefully the structure of the body as well as principles of physiology. Not only are diet and sleep, etc., placed under careful control, but the muscles, ligaments, and bones are carefully studied so as to best cooperate with the principles, or laws, governing their function. The more perfectly a person understands and cooperates with the laws of nature, the greater the freedom in athletic feats.

## My Crime: Identifying Freedom with Laws of Nature

I worked at this day and night and, because of circumstances, turned them all in at once. When Dr. Parkinson returned them, I knew I was in big trouble. The massive amount of red ink and huge exclamation marks spoke their own language—especially with shorter "skid" marks at the end of long vertical lines, in a striking action that spoke vividly of an angry hand. I had dealt a solar plexus blow by challenging Darwin on the basis of natural law, for in this he clearly saw an implied Creator, yet knew not how to refute this scientific response. He could accommodate communism, for, despite its lack of freedom, it operates on evolutionary principles, but he could not tolerate a concept of freedom that silently testified to a Creator.

My crime was in daring to meet Parkinson's concept of Darwinian freedom by proposing that true freedom consists in observing the principles of nature. Going to him, I acknowledged that he found my work unacceptable. He agreed, but expressed pity for me, as trapped by religion which robbed me of the ability to think objectively, thus disqualifying me from doing doctoral work. In his view, the concept of a Creator made freedom impossible, since it implied authority that precluded freedom to think for myself.

When he ran out of steam, I asked, "But what do you suggest?"

He responded, "Do another paper."

"I cannot do another paper," I replied, "without using the same principles."

To this he made the most amazing and un-academic suggestion: "Well, then, do a superficial paper."

## How is One to Do a Superficial Doctoral Paper!?

What? A superficial paper to pacify a professor who proclaimed absolute freedom but denied freedom to believe in a Creator whose principles set us free? Who now was incapable of objective thinking? Parkinson's thinking was so controlled by subjective philosophy that, even as he demanded objectivity, he repudiated the most fundamental rule of science—dependence on natural law! A "superficial" academic paper indeed! How is it done?

I should have challenged him. But, seeing an impenetrable subjective reasoning that could not honor objective reality, I decided to do what he asked—not realizing I could not. Week after week I tried. But how could I write an honest, superficial paper I could live with? Amazingly, what seemed only a great waste of precious time would lead me to a valuable discovery.

At the end of the term I had no more idea what to do than I did at the first. I had no recourse but to request an incomplete. But that was by no means a solution. I had already wasted weeks in vain. How could I, on leaving, know what to do to remove the incomplete and be free to proceed with my dissertation?

The irony was that, after completing all required work, I had already spent more than the time I had spent completing the assignment just spinning my wheels. He did not question the quality of my work. However, because it repudiated his Darwinian theory in a way he could not answer, I was forced into research that forcefully illustrates the dialectical problem of modern science. That problem is now forcing the whole world to the brink of the eternal precipice by subjective claims that repudiate the Creator. Ironically, until the message of the Creator was rejected, the world's leading scientists—such as Isaac Newton—had been directed in their research by belief in the Creator and faith in the consistency of His laws.

Still facing a blank wall, I came to the last session with feelings of despair. Then suddenly, these feelings gave way to great relief as Parkinson unwittingly gave me the needed clue to a solution as he announced that he got his concept from Sir Karl Popper.

# —Chapter 4—
## Slavery to Darwinian Freedom

*"I say this in order that no man may delude you with beguiling speech."*
—*Colossians 2:4, RSV.*

As I boarded the plane for California, I finally knew how to get started on a paper for Dr. Parkinson. It would take a great deal more time, but at least I could quit spinning my wheels.

At that time (1978), Popper was honored as one of the greatest men of the twentieth century and foremost in developing scientific philosophy. Indeed, he virtually reigned as "king" over science and philosophy, having married the two in bonds of unholy matrimony, giving subjective philosophical theory authority to interpret objective scientific evidence subjectively.

Thus, to science based on concrete observations or experiments, Popper added philosophy as a "source of truth," rather than merely a means of evaluating truth. Interpretations were now accorded the same status as the scientific findings themselves. But this was not a marriage between equal parties. By its interpretive nature, philosophy becomes the "head" of the union, with power to control acceptable interpretation of the scientific evidence.

Sir Karl Popper (1902-1994)

Actually, Popper only served as an authority to justify—even consecrate—a long standing "common law marriage" that became an accepted union in the wake of Darwin, whose philosophy was increasingly adopted as scientific. Evolution was thus legitimized as the only way to interpret scientific evidence. Popper, a philosopher, was welcomed by scientists because his marriage legitimized their evolutionary offspring and their requirement that everything be explained by "natural processes."

That marriage was made possible by dialectical thinking, which trains one how to subordinate one principle of truth to another. Thus, though appearing to be honored, science is actually controlled by evolutionary philosophy. Such dialectical thinking can only be overcome by intense focus on Christ, our Creator, in whom converse principles of truth unite in perfect balance. This is the essence of the first angel's call to worship the Creator and its warning against creature worship. The first angel calls for a break in the "unholy" bond between science and philosophy which imposes the philosophical interpretation of evolution on scientific findings. Indeed, the message of the first angel contains a direct reference to the fourth commandment, and that commandment declares a six-day creation. As we will later see, the principles given through the "Minneapolis message" amplify the call of the first angel to worship the Creator by calling mankind to focus upon Christ, the Creator.

## Veatch Protests Illicit Union of Science and Philosophy

As I contemplated Popper's illicit union, my mind went back to *Two Logics* and Veatch's protest of Popper's marriage between science and philosophy—a union which degrades objective science into subjective philosophy, parading in the guise of objective proof. As Veatch argued, scientific philosophy—by contrast with science—denies reality by refusing even to discuss any "what" questions, such as *What is this?* Or, *what is that?* Science is obliged to only ask "why" questions.[5]

When applied to history, "what happened" gives way to "why" questions that move the historian from his commitment to factual reality to philosophical speculation, thus removing objectivity from history. The result is a re-writing of history to conform to culture-bound philosophy that subverts reality because its evolutionary base denies the reality of truth. Truth, it holds, is forever becoming and thus never becomes. Reality cannot be declared a "what," because there are only ever-changing perceptions of reality.

If truth never arrives but is always in the process of arriving, one cannot honor objective truth, but is left to conform everything to evolutionary perception. By contrast, one who believes in a Creator seeks to know the facts, as science itself has historically done, for, though it is blurred and confused by sin, truth is the reality of "what" exists, thus "what" God has created.

By contrast, Creationists neither deny nor discount "why" questions. But, "why" questions have no meaning until we determine "what." Until we know "what" exists, how can we know "why"? Without knowing "what" is real, to ask "why" can only mislead. Until we know the "what," the answer to "why" is only one's own speculation and does not relate to reality itself.

I thus decided to pit Veatch's *Two Logics* against Popper, even though, as an evolutionist also, Veatch could neither trace the dialectical problem to its evolutionary root nor suggest creation as a solution. But he did clearly recognize the effects of perverting objective history by subjective philosophy which is presumed to be objective. To subordinate objective science to subjective philosophy is to prevent

---

5    In challenging Popper, Henry B. Veatch (*Two Logics: The Conflict Between Classical and Neo-analytic Philosophy*, Evanston: Northwestern University Press, 1969) makes it clear that in denying reality and thus the "what" questions, Popper denies the very freedom he seeks to defend.

history and science from reflecting factual objectivity. *Two Logics* thus protests a marriage of philosophy with science, history, and all other branches of factual knowledge. Such unions prevent us from recognizing reality or truly examining "what" is.

## Polak's *Image of the Future* Challenges Popper

As I thought of Parkinson's opposition to all "myths" and utopian concepts, because they serve as authoritarian interferences with the natural evolution of life—a concept hostile to Bible prophecy's divine portrayals of the future—my mind went back to another book I had read in an earlier class. In a challenge that goes straight to the heart of Parkinson's protest against educational interference with evolution's natural freedom, Frederick W. Polak's *The Image of the Future* presents startling evidence that modern loss of images of the future (regarding human progress) threatens civilization with utter chaos.

Polak vividly describes the chaotic results in the modern art, music, and poetry of a generation in regression because it has lost its images of the future. With great urgency he calls for their restoration before it is too late. Thus, while Parkinson denounces images of the future because they impact the course of history, Polak demonstrates the chaotic results of losing images of the future.

Since all three authors held evolutionary concepts, I could use each to expose weaknesses in the other two without referring to natural law.

## A Slave to Darwinian Freedom

Ironically, I was forced to take this long detour because a professor was so enslaved to a Darwinian concept of freedom that he was not free to honor science's most basic principles. Thus he declared that my argument for freedom by observing principles of natural law disqualified me for objective, academic work! But, is not natural law the essence of science? Of course! Yet, any appeal to science that testifies to a Creator was considered intolerable; for this introduces authority. And to Parkinson, authority is the cause of all societal ills!

Restricted by his inability to face implications of the most basic law of science, I headed for the library to find a way to escape the impact on me of his unwitting slavery. There I found Popper's two volumes of *The Open Society and Its Enemies*. Volume I deals with Plato as the father of dialectic thinking; Volume II introduces Hegel as its modern apostle, whose "historical dialecticism" laid the foundation for communism.

After pitting the three authors against each other in a way to refute Darwinism, with no allusion to natural law, I dared to follow my summary with a concluding paragraph identifying freedom with the principles of nature. When I returned to

NYU to defend my dissertation, I picked up my paper. Without a smile or word of greeting, Parkinson handed it to me and turned away. How totally open to any human theory can one be who denies divine authority, just so there is no connection to a Creator! Yet he did give me a B. I had never received a doctoral grade other than an A, and that with a fraction of the work. But I expected no more. And he did not want to give me less for fear it would prompt an appeal to the academic dean.

## *Open Society* Suggests 'Dialectical' as the Antonym to 'Paradoxical'

Meanwhile, in reading *The Open Society*, I discovered that Popper's key purpose was to expose the 'dialectical' processes of Plato and Hegel, and it occurred to me that 'dialectical' is precisely the term I needed to express the violation of paradoxical principles. Though the term has varied definitions and uses, history confirms its valid use as an antonym to paradox. (See Appendix A.)

# Chapter 5

# Plato, Father of Dialectical Subversion

*"Beware lest any man spoil you through philosophy and vain deceit, ... and not after Christ." —Colossians 2:8.*

In Volume I of *The Open Society*, Popper identifies Plato as the father of dialectics. Plato had been a disciple of Socrates from age 20, in 408 B.C., until the death of his teacher in 399 B.C. Though Plato betrays his teacher's democratic principle, his dialectics are known as "the Socratic method" of reasoning.

Plato portrays Socrates as teaching his students through questioning. By one question and answer after another, Plato pits democratic and oligarchical principles against each other in a constant clash of opposing ideas that appear to evolve to ever higher levels of thought. Through the voice of Socrates, renowned martyr for democracy, Plato appears to defend democracy and freedom. First he eloquently defends democracy; then he defends the oligarchical, caste system. Back and forth it goes, from defending democracy, to opposing it. One of my graduate professors was so charmed by the beauty of his expressions of goodness and freedom that he repeatedly eulogized Plato as a great, pre-Christian "Christian," never realizing that his rhetoric was but a clever ploy to hide his real agenda.

Popper shows that behind his beautiful imagery lies a sinister purpose—to destroy the new democracy and restore the ruling oligarchy, of which his family was a member. Plato confuses readers by his endless pitting of democratic and oligarchic "languages" against each other. In discussions of goodness which he equates with justice, Plato finally defines goodness as the state of freedom when the ruler rules, the warrior wars, the worker works, and the slave slaves. Indeed, he holds it immoral for any member of society to transfer from one class to another.

After incessant "sleight of tongue" tricks, Plato boldly declares the ruler's duty. By all means—including force and outright lies—he must preserve society's purity by preventing any violation of the caste system! Thus, by clever dialectic dialogue through the mouth of Socrates—who drank deadly hemlock rather than to surrender his democratic ideal—Plato seeks to so mesmerize his readers that they do not realize that he is undermining the very democracy he pretends to defend and to so brilliantly eulogize.

## For Plato, Goodness Equals Justice, and
## Justice Means to Keep Your Place

Thus, Plato deliberately developed dialectical processes by pitting two political philosophies against each other, democracy and a caste system. Appearing to defend democracy, he ultimately drove his propaganda knife into its very heart. Such clever dialectical manipulation is the basis of all propaganda.

Plato's defense of authoritarianism and class privilege is revealed in his teaching that *justice means keeping your place; temperance is knowing your place; and happiness is the product of justice and temperance—knowing and keeping your place.* Thus justice, temperance, and happiness are but catch words for the promotion of injustice, class rule, and slavery.

In discussing Plato's arrogant attitude toward slaves, Popper declares:

*... Plato has only scorn for those "tenderhearted" Athenian democrats who supported the abolitionist movement. And he makes his view quite clear ... he says of the timocratic man: "He will be inclined to treat slaves cruelly, for he does not despise them as much as a well-educated man would." —Karl Popper, Open Society and its Enemies, vol. I, p. 90 (see also pp. 98, 169, 44).*

Plato also says: "We have stated and repeated over and over again that each man in our city should do one work only: namely that work for which he is naturally best fitted." He then identifies injustice as a worker getting "into the warrior class" or a warrior getting "into the [ruling class]" (Popper, p. 199). Popper also quotes Plato as declaring cynically, "Democracy is born ... when the poor win the day, killing some ... banishing others, and sharing with the rest the rights of citizenship and of public offices, on terms of equality ..." (Popper, p. 41)

As the father of idealism, Plato claimed that reality resides not in things themselves but in forms or ideas of things. Thus, this famous pupil of **Socrates** denies objective reality in favor of the subjective philosophy of invisible reality.[6]

## Plato's Allegory of "the Cave"

One of the best illustrations of Plato's dialectic processes is "the Cave," where invisible reality is pitted against visible 'shadows.' Here visible 'things' are declared to be the only unreal shadows of invisible 'ideas' or 'forms.'

We are asked to imagine prisoners bound from childhood deep within a cave. Not only are their limbs bound by chains so they cannot move; their heads are also immobilized. They can only look at the wall in front of them. Behind them a bright

---

6   By contrast, Plato's student, Aristotle, identified reality with things, rather than ideas. Both converse philosophies pervade modern Babylon's society in a dialecticism of never-ending confusion.

fire burns and, on a raised walkway between them and the fire, plant and animal puppets are moved. Echoes bouncing from the wall in front of them thus appear to come from the shadows.

In this state, the prisoners know nothing real. They know only the shadows of unreal puppets and sounds made by puppet manipulators. In time they develop a game of who can first identify the shadows and predict which ones will next emerge. The quick are highly honored; but the slow are depreciated. Values are determined by visual and auditory non-realities.

A released prisoner who is made to turn around and see the puppets is bewildered. These do not seem real; and he sees no relation between them and the shadows. When first brought into the sunlight, he is blinded by the sun. But, as he begins to see things about him, he eventually is able to see the sun and finally recognize it as the cause of all that exists. (Thus, the sun appears to be Plato's god.)

Seeing that shadows are merely distorted reflections and not the reality he once assumed, he returns to the cave to inform the prisoners; but they do not believe him. Indeed, because he can no longer see clearly in the darkness, they think he has lost his sight. Because the prisoners cherish their shadows as realities they neither envision anything beyond, nor can they know reality. All humans are thus portrayed as prisoners in a cave. The cave represents the tangible things of the world that we perceive but that are mere shadows on a wall. In this contrast between 'things' and 'ideas,' the last thing to be seen is the idea of "good." And the conclusion is that "good" is the cause of all that is right and beautiful in the visible world. Yet, his real meaning lies in his claim that justice, temperance and happiness mean that each man knows and keeps his place in the caste system.

Despite some real meaning in this allegory, Plato misses the point. The Creator is the Source of all good. And His creatures are actual realities and not mere shadows of reality.

# —Chapter 6—

# Hegel Fathers Communism and Darwinian Capitalism

*"... worship him that made heaven, and earth, and the sea, and the fountains of waters. And there followed another angel, saying, Babylon is fallen, is fallen ..." —Revelation 14:7, 8.*

Georg Wilhelm
Fredrich Hegel
(1770-1831)

Georg Wilhelm Friedrich Hegel changed the course of modern history by proclaiming his "dialectical historicism." In it he saw conflict between the two poles of truth as the essence of historical progress. Instead of restoring the inner unity of fractured truth, he idealized its fracture. Through his influence the conflict that sin imposes upon carnal minds is declared a universal norm and the only path to progress!

The formula commonly associated with Hegel's evolutionary *historical dialecticism* is well known—a given thesis (assumption, theory, etc.) always arouses an opposite antithesis; these remain in conflict until one conquers and subsumes or subordinates the other; but this synthesis becomes a new thesis which stimulates another antithesis. (The formula itself is attributed to J. G. Fichte [1762–1814].) In this never-ending conflict between theses and antitheses with periodic syntheses, he saw a guarantee of evolutionary progress.[7]

Hegel's theory precludes truth in two ways: in repudiating the Creator, he denied the Holy Spirit who alone can reveal truth's unity; by denying the reality of sin, he saw the constant conflict between the two balancing poles of truth as the ultimate good, the basis for never-ceasing evolution. Such a formula makes evil the essence of good. When creatures repudiate the Creator, the conflict that sin enforces between the poles of truth is identified as ever-expanding understanding! Insanity and death are thus hailed as wisdom, progress, and life!

Sadly, Hegel's denial of the essence of truth soon became the accepted scientific view and spawned communism's *dialectical materialism* which denies spiritual reality. After all, if there is only endless, mindless pitting of forces against each other, how can one believe in a Creator or in any spiritual reality?

---

7   Far from discovering an engine of evolutionary progress, Hegel merely observed the effect of sin in restraining real progress by fracturing truth. Carnal man's inevitable focus upon one of two converse principles which the Creator designed to function as one became his norm. Denying the divine Author, within whom truth forms a harmonious unity, he introduced his own god—evolution by perpetual conflict!

Thus, communism's leaders stirred the proletariat to demand equality in material possessions, as the sole source of value, and to rise up and seize the wealth accumulated by capitalists. The result was internal revolution and international war. Whether in politics or in the church the inevitable result of taking part-truth for the whole is a war of languages, cultures, and often even armies.

By Plato's manipulation of language in dialectical processes idealized by Hegel, communist leaders led the people into mass servitude through their talk of freedom. By propaganda techniques pitting one pole of truth against another to destroy the very principle proclaimed, they convinced the people that they must escape the "slavery" of western democracy by embracing communism.

## Are Communist Leaders Secret Capitalists?

While communist Russia denounces democratic capitalism and claims to be a great defender of freedom, a news item in *The New York Times* of Dec. 21, 2008 reveals how at least some Communist leaders develop their own brand of capitalism, enslaving the masses to provide massive amounts of capital for themselves. We are acquainted with the billions stored up by capitalists, but the *Times* portrays the same surfeiting by communist leaders. The title tells it all—"Upheaval in the East: Hidden Wealth; Disclosures of the Ceausescus' Riches Appall Many Threadbare Rumanians." The article begins:

*From drippingly fat bank accounts in Switzerland to meat scales made of gold, the reported plunder and greed of Nicolae Ceausescu and his family is starting to be laid before a shocked and disgusted Rumanian people. ...*

*An indictment before a military tribunal that had led to their execution accused the Communist dictator and his wife, Elena, of having salted away more than $1 billion in foreign bank accounts. ...[8]*

---

8    The *New York Times* acknowledges dispute over the amount; but whatever the sum, there is no question of sumptuous living by an astonishingly wealthy class while the populace was in dire poverty. Mentioning that it was "widely known that Mr. Ceausescu had countless houses across the country, often well-tended estates, that he might have visited once a year ...

"One videotaped broadcast ... took viewers inside a sumptuous house outside Bucharest belonging to Mr. Ceausescu's daughter, Zoia, a mathematician now in military custody.

"... Inside, soldiers took viewers on a brief tour of several rooms, including the kitchen, where they had found a solid gold meat scale. On it, they placed another discovery—a package of imported veal, which the voiceover said was intended for Miss Ceausescu's dogs."

## Darwinianism: As Much a Child of Hegel As Communism

Charles Darwin

While Popper traces dialectical "science" from Plato and exposes historical dialecticism as democracy's mortal enemy, identifying Hegel as the father of Communism, his own Darwinian theory is as much a child of Hegel's dialecticism as is communism. He fails to see that Darwin's "survival of the fittest" philosophy also drew its evolutionary theory from Hegel via his disciple, Charles Lyell.

As a defender of both Darwin and capitalism, Popper could not see that communism and capitalism (stimulated by Darwin) are but contrary political languages inspired by Hegel! Thus, the real enemy is in pitting truth's principles against each other, instead of uniting them.

Hegel's legitimising of conflict between polar principles as the path to progress fostered two great political systems that war against each other as each seeks to enforce its own imbalanced language upon the other. It is the "dog eat dog" of capitalism that makes the false rhetoric of communism and its promise of equality and freedom attractive. As did Plato, Marxists claim to defend democratic ideals, and Russia's communist regime is denominated a republic!

## Surrender of Objective Science to Subjective Philosophy

We will see how scientists, who presume to represent ultimate objective authority and whose views penetrate virtually all other branches of knowledge, surrender objective scientific findings to the subjective authority of philosophy. So subjectively bound by dialectical thinking are many scientists that they are incapable of honoring their own objective principles. Just now, as I am preparing this book for publication, the intensity with which they seek to prevent open discussion of Creationism is illustrated by an Associated Press news article, "Zoo Cancels Ticket Deal with Creation Museum," published December 6, 2008.

Note the extended sub-heading: "The Cincinnati Zoo has canceled a joint ticket promotion with the nearby Creation Museum in Kentucky, which presents the Bible's version of natural history." The article begins:

*Some scientists and bloggers had complained that the zoo should not work with a religious museum that rejects the theory of evolution.*[9]

---

9   "It is agreed that both organizations talk 'about animals and animal behavior,' but opponents 'disagree is [*sic*] when they talk about the origin of the animals—where they

To the majority of leading scientists, Intelligent Design (or "ID")—the pre-Darwin basis for all science—is anathema. Indeed, to acknowledge ID is politically dangerous to a scientist's reputation, prospects of publication, and even employment. Massive efforts have been and still are put forth to make it illegal to present Intelligent Design as an option to Darwinism in public schools.

came from in the first place—which is not observational science.'" So it is acceptable to talk about origins so long as it is attributed to an unseen evolutionary process for which a century and a half of scientific effort has produced not even one evidence? And such speculation is scientific so long as a Creator is not posited or implied?

# —Chapter 7—
# Lucifer, the Original Propagandist

*"But I fear, lest somehow, as the serpent deceived Eve by his craftiness, so your minds may be corrupted from the simplicity that is in Christ." —2 Corinthians 11:3, NKJV.*

W hile Plato is known as the father of dialectics, he was not its originator, nor was he the first to use it to deceive. Dialectical thinking is as old as sin. The real pioneer and engineer in developing the technique of pitting truth against truth was Lucifer, and this before human history.[10]

Only in fracturing truth into diverse segments could he deceive, by making unreality appear real and reality appear unreal. By cleverly isolating words and acts of Christ from their context and intent, Lucifer moved in two ways to deceive a third of the angels. By part-truth he first suggested interpretations that appeared to defend Christ, but that distorted what He said. Then, when they were sufficiently confused, he finally did what Plato and Communism would eventually do; he boldly and effectively repudiated Christ as their enslaver and portrayed himself as their deliverer.

---

10 By no means are all who use dialectic processes devious. The questioning process in a cross examination of opposite principles is considered an effective way to probe issues and to teach. But, according to Popper, Plato's purpose was both political and devious (as was Lucifer's). He points out that his beautiful portrayals of democracy and freedom are actually part of a deliberate process to confuse and prepare minds to repudiate democracy. For he finally concludes by defending the oligarchy, insisting that rulers must lie and deceive as necessary to retain their ruling position, preserving the ruling class. The highest civic and moral duty of the ruling class was to prevent the lower class from getting into the ruling class. Popper quotes Plato as declaring:

*Whether they happen to rule by law or without the law, over willing or unwilling subjects; … and whether they purge the state for its good, by killing or by deporting some of its citizens, … so long as they proceed according to science and justice, and preserve … the state and make it better than it was, this form of government must be declared the only one that is right ( ibid, 166).*

Moreover, Plato concludes his constant focus on justice and happiness in an 'ideal' state by claiming that temperance is knowing your place, justice is keeping your place, and happiness combines temperance and justice. Thus the ideal state of justice and happiness is to know and keep your place!

## Satan's Part-Truth Lies

To meet Lucifer's charges, God must allow every intelligent creature to freely decide whether or not to trust Him. To provide this choice, God placed two trees "in the midst of the garden." By eating only of the tree of life in trusting obedience, they could make that choice without facing part-truth deception. This was because Satan was restricted to the tree of knowledge of good and evil, a symbol of the nature of evil which is always a perversion of good. Unfortunately, Eve, by curiosity, chose to face part-truth lies and was deceived; and Adam by fear joined her in the choice to become evil by experiencing evil, perverting his own nature. So perverted was their nature that they immediately began to think dialectically, using part-truth as a means of self-defense. (See Gen. 3:12, 13.)

Satan's first lie involved three part-truths—"Ye shall not surely die . . . Ye shall be as *gods* (Heb. *Elohim)*, and you shall know "good and evil" (Gen. 3:5). Evidence for these claims seemed overwhelming. For unreality appeared to be more real than reality itself. The talking serpent did not die upon eating; instead he appeared to "acquire" superior powers. Neither did Eve die upon eating; instead the "good" (fruit) she knew became the agent of evil. In choosing to worship self they did not become *Elohim*; but they did become "gods," for self-worship is the basis for all idolatry. The truth is they did immediately come to know evil. But except for a miracle of grace they could never again know good. Indeed good would became so confused with evil that they could never naturally distinguish between the two. Thus, evil would be called good and good evil.

Adam and Eve were soon terrified to learn what perverting good so that it becomes evil meant. Far from becoming "*Elohim*,"[11] Adam and Eve became devils—adversaries of God and man. And they did die that day. So real was their death on separating from the source of life that to live they would have to be born again.[12]

---

11    By rendering *Elohim* in the plural ("gods") in this verse, but translating the same identical noun as singular in Gen. 1:1 ("God"), the KJV obscures the full impact of Satan's blasphemous offer that they would become *Elohim*, a plural term used 31 times for the Creator in the first chapter of the Bible. Gen. 1:1 says: "In the beginning *Elohim* created." Indeed, in the very verse where they are promised they would become *Elohim*, the serpent declares, "for *Elohim* doth know" (Gen. 3:5), referring to the godhead. Thus, Adam and Eve are assured that they will also form a godhead—just like the Creator God.

12    Actually, *beyom*, translated, "in the day" does not necessarily mean that something took place within the span of a literal day (*yom*). As a phrase, it is often better translated into English by the generic "when," as in Genesis 2:5, "*When* God created the heavens and the earth," instead of "In the day that God created the heavens and the earth." The account of the creation tells that it wasn't created in a single day.

Truth's integrity depends upon holding both paradoxical elements in proper relation. When Eve sinned, even biological death immediately set in. Although it would take hundreds of years to become fully evident, that very moment death processes within Eve's mind began to invade her very cells.

The excitement that the short-circuiting of her nerves produced, as seen in her glowing face, appeared to be intensified life. Yet it was to prove like a light bulb whose filament suddenly burns with intense brightness only to suddenly go out. Nevertheless, the vitality with which Adam and Eve were created permitted them to live nearly a millennium before they met the mercy of physical death and were released from the unceasing conflict between their now corrupt, self-centered natures and the new birth nature they could experience only by faith in the Lamb.[13]

As soon as Adam and Eve sinned, Satan changed his dialectical tactics and fixed in their minds his distortion of the opposite pole of truth. Having assured them there was no danger, he now, with a sinister, "gotcha" delight, charged them with sin and left them condemned before the part-truth distortion of God's absolute justice. In terror and hopelessness, they tried at first to hide from God and then they attempted to justify themselves. Sin so changed Adam's nature that, only hours after choosing to die with Eve, rather than being separated from her, he tried to escape death by casting the blame for his sin upon both her and God. In self-defense he charged, "The woman you gave me … she gave me … and I did eat" (Gen. 3:12).

## Truth's Two Poles: Material 'Thing' and Immaterial 'Idea'

The conflict between good and evil that began on earth with Satan's dialectical deception is soon to climax in the restoration of the paradoxical principles of whole truth given in Minneapolis message. In those who unite principles of law and grace in mind and heart by focusing upon Christ, that law will be translated into loving, obedient actions that will prepare them to give the 'loud cry.' Those who continue their dialectical languages, meanwhile, will endure the seven last plagues.

It is "high time" for us "to awake out of sleep" (Rom. 13:11) and grasp the nature of whole truth and understand the ways in which Satan fractures it. Truth remains

---

13  Of course, it was not natural physical vitality alone that permitted Adam and Eve to live such long lives. They were sustained during that time as we are—by the God they had betrayed. Every breath Adam drew during his 930 years was drawn by the grace of God, Who was faithful to His covenant of life. The whole race came under the sentence of death; but Christ's own commitment to die permitted Him to allot to all a probationary period in which to choose to accept His sacrifice, typified by the lamb. Those who accepted Him as their Substitute became His witnesses and emissaries to help save others. Yet He mercifully permitted death to release his servants from the unceasing conflict between their now corrupt, self-centered natures and the new birth nature they could experience only by faith in the Lamb.

true only when it is whole. Our challenge is thus to have truth's unity restored in our habitual thinking.

At present, we tend to reflect either Plato or Aristotle. Plato denied the reality of the 'thing,' declaring it merely a shadow of the real—its 'idea.' Aristotle, by contrast, denied the reality of the 'idea' and, as a father of materialism, proclaimed the 'thing' the only reality. Though we would not go so far as did they in denying the Creator who produced all 'things' according to His own 'idea,' we still tend to eat of the dialectical tree of good and evil, as did they.

It was such fractured truth that brought about the Minneapolis crisis and that continues to be an issue in Adventism to this day. James's "law of liberty" (tangible law and intangible liberty) illustrates the nature of paradoxical truth which we unwittingly fracture. Some threaten the liberty with which James identifies law by focusing upon external obedience; others threaten law itself by a dialectical focus upon faith that is reduced to lifeless, abstract, permissive belief.

So pervasive is paradoxical truth that not only do major principles of truth require two poles for unity, so also do particular aspects of truth. There is never an inside without an outside. When detached from its balancing pole, every truth becomes a vehicle for error, for every isolated element is capable of use in unwitting error or in deliberate deception.

The effectiveness of one such method of deception is illustrated by the communistic subversion of freedom by subtle redefinition of terms. Only in becoming acquainted with western democracy have the communist masses begun to comprehend their enslavement by slogans of the "people's power" that so distort reality as to place power in the hands of rulers who rule only by robbing the *people* of their *power*.

It doesn't take communism to subvert democracy. Democracy can also be subverted indirectly and unwittingly by a dialectical focus on individual freedom, such as that which Dr. Parkinson insisted upon. That kind of liberty paves the way for anarchist concepts which destroy the democratic processes and the freedom they ostensibly promote. Either way, authoritarianism displaces democracy.

# —Chapter 8—
# The Three Angels vs. Evolutionary Thought

*"And I saw another angel fly in the midst of heaven, having the everlasting gospel to preach unto them that dwell on the earth, ... Saying with a loud voice, Fear God, and give glory to him; for the hour of his judgment is come: and worship him that made the heaven, and the earth. ... And the third angel followed them, saying with a loud voice, If any man worship the beast ... the same shall drink ... of the wrath of God." —Revelation 14:6, 7, 9, 10.*

In the final analysis, Parkinson's "freedom" turns out not to be freedom at all, but blind subjective bondage. Indeed, in denying law, he unwittingly enjoins a "law" of evolution based on the "god" of chance and "survival of the fittest." In denying the Creator, he cannot accept that freedom rests upon heeding principles written within nature and in our very being. True freedom and the law of internal design form a paradoxical unity so vital that one cannot exist without the other.[14]

Neither pole of truth can exist alone, but must be held in tension with the other. Each depends on and is understandable only in the context of the other. Such a view does not compromise truth. Indeed, the validation of both poles of truth protects their full meaning. Unless the converse principles are integrated, truth ceases to be true, and we are left imbalanced and in danger of heresy.

Failure to hold paradoxical elements in unity is the mother of all heresies. Heresy does not generally begin with frank error and falsehood, but with an imbalanced focus on one pole of truth, which, in belittling the balancing side, is itself distorted. For example, God gives man freedom to determine his own destiny; yet, He also works in and through individuals and societies to fulfill His own divine purposes. The singular focus on either human freedom or divine sovereignty fails to honor their unity. Thus, in muting the other, the one defended is itself perverted, for its very meaning is dependent upon its unity with the other!

It was the singular focus on *divine sovereignty* that inspired Augustine's predestination. Though declaring his belief in the *freedom of choice*, he denied its reality. This part-truth distortion has led to numerous heresies. Both it and they have plagued the church from Augustine's time till now. Calvin's systematization

---

14    For example, the athlete is free to reach his potential only as he observes the respective laws of body, mind, and physics. Ignorance or denial of these laws limits and may even destroy his freedom of movement.

of the dialectic concept of absolute, divine control, in which God pre-determines the destiny of all men, has influenced a great deal of Protestant discussion since the sixteenth century.[15]

Resisting the call to judgment and to worship of the Creator, both Protestants and Catholics have moved from the confusion of deterministic predestination to submission to scientific philosophy which engenders theistic evolution—the theory that God created the world through the process of evolution. They repeat the error pointed out by Peter, "Since the fathers fell asleep, all things continue as they were from the beginning of the creation" (2 Pet. 3:4). Willing to disregard the plain teaching of the Bible on the world's origin, many professed Christians take the next logical step and jettison their belief in the Creator.

## Three Angels' Messages vs. Universal
## Dialectical Evolution (Theist and Atheist)

To restore truth's unity, the first angel's message challenges predestinarian determinism by announcing a judgment based on human choices, and challenges evolution by a call to worship the Creator. As this message began to sound, a two-fold Hegelian reaction immunized the intellectual world and virtually all society against the Creator and His judgment. This called forth the second and third angels' messages, which will be proclaimed in greater clarity and power as predicted in the 'loud cry' of Revelation 18.

*"And after these things I saw another angel come down from heaven, having great power; and the earth was lightened with his glory. And he cried mightily with a strong voice, saying, Babylon the great is fallen, is fallen, and is become the habitation of devils, and the hold of every foul spirit, and a cage of every unclean and hateful bird. … And I heard another voice from heaven, saying, Come out of her, my people, that ye be not partakers of her sins, and that ye receive not of her plagues." —Revelation 18:1, 2, 4.*

In splitting truth into mutually hostile "languages," Hegel spawned two great enemies of the Creator's message: Marxism's atheistic evolution and capitalism's theistic evolution. By the intensity of their conflict, these soon came to dominate all society. Through Marx, Hegel prepared eastern Europe to reject the Creator's message, and through Lyell and Darwin, the western world rejected the message as well.

---

15   South Africa's former apartheid system is an example of its socio-political distortion. Calvin's theory of divine decrees of predestination engendered belief that Gen. 9:25 mandates that the black race be servants, thus many considered it the duty of rulers to enforce this system of inequality.

Ironically, Popper's protest against Hegel's all-pervasive, *dialectical historicism* so focuses on its product in Marx's manipulative *dialectical materialism* that he himself pits one pole of truth against the other, failing to see the real problem— the splitting of paradoxical truth into warring dialectical languages. Moreover, if Parkinson is to represent him correctly, Popper did not recognize his own Hegelian role in pitting the subjective and abstract concept of freedom, based on Darwin's unproven and un-provable evolution, against communism's objectivism.[16]

## Satan's Master Stroke—Penetrating Early Adventism with a Language of Law

By inciting the universal defense of the competing *part-truth* systems of capitalism and communism, Satan has sought to lock all mankind into opposite, warring camps that preclude the wholeness of the judgment-hour truth and its command to worship the Creator.

Even more, Satan's master stroke of evil genius was to penetrate Adventism itself, in our early history, with a language of law and then to thwart God's Christ-centered correction at Minneapolis in 1888. As a result, we exchanged one dialectical language for two. The language of the letter of the law continued, but it is now in conflict with an imbalanced focus on grace. Each extreme acknowledges some truth in both paradoxical elements, but they unite only in undermining the paradoxical principle of truth.

Of course, I am not speaking of all Seventh-day Adventists. Many have always earnestly sought the balanced integration of law and grace, and there are numerous degrees of view from far right to far left. Thankfully, there is evidence of increasing focus upon the paradoxical acceptance of both.

## Paradoxical Thinking Unites Truth's Poles, Dialecticism Puts them in Conflict

Some ask how to balance such and such a philosophy with an opposing one. The answer is, you don't! Balanced principles of truth have nothing to do with balancing philosophies. Human philosophies always split truth. The combining of human philosophies only results in dialectical synthesis, which, in turn, produces a new, dialectical thesis to be attacked by a dialectical antithesis.

It is the poles of truth that harmonize—not philosophies—and these poles can only unite in Christ. Unless we see truth in relation to Christ, we cannot properly grasp its unity. This was the essence of the Minneapolis message, which amplified

---

16  Actually, against Plato's subjectivity Popper intensely insists on objectivity; but he betrays his own position by marrying science and philosophy, thus ending up with a subjectivist perspective.

the Laodicean call to behold Christ (Rev. 3:14–18) and the three angels' call to worship and to proclaim Christ as Creator and Source of all truth (Rev. 14:6–12).

Of course, all philosophies contain some truth. If they didn't, they would not command anyone's allegiance. Yet, it is only to the degree that any philosophy harmonizes converse principles of truth that it is either valid or paradoxical. Without proper harmonization, it can only distort the truth.

A symptom of the reign of sin is the splitting of truth's principles. Conversely, *paradoxical thinking seeks to determine the underlying unity between truth's principles* on the basis of God's Word. The unity of truth is central to Laodicea's straight testimony from the faithful and True Witness and to the three angels' call to worship Him.

# —Chapter 9—
# Plato, Aristotle, and Papal Languages Exposed

*"In the beginning was the Word, and the Word was with God, and the Word was God. ... All things were made by him. ... And the Word was made flesh ... and we beheld his glory, the glory as of the only begotten of the Father, full of grace and truth." —John 1:1, 3, 14.*

P lato's identification of reality as the 'idea' behind the 'thing' would have been correct, had he only located the 'idea' in the mind of the Creator. This would have given a true concept of the 'idea' and prevented him from denying the reality of the 'thing.' This is because the idea of every creature—every 'thing'—lies in

Plato

the mind of the Creator who sustains and maintains its reality. Regrettably, in identifying truth with only its abstract idea, Plato split truth and pitted 'ideas' as true reality against 'things,' which only appear to be real. Thus, he imposed dialectical processes upon the divine and human elements of truth and provided the basis for all heresy.

Though appearing to recognize the dipolar nature of truth, Plato actually denied the reality of both parts. He elevates the intangible 'idea' or 'form' to the point of denying the reality of the tangible 'thing,' calling it a mere shadow of the idea. The source of reality is not intangible 'idea,' but a Creator in whose mind the 'ideas' formed, and by whom all 'things' were brought into real existence. Thus, all 'split truths' deny the truth.

It was the splitting of truth that spawned the concept of docetism,[17] which early penetrated the Christian church, causing many to deny the reality of Christ's humanity. It is also the splitting of truth that spawned the Platonic concept that

---

17   Docetism is a term derived from the Greek, *dokeô,* "to seem." It means something that has an *appearance* of reality, though not real. As a modern example, "Christian Science asserts that, correctly understood, humanity and the universe as a whole are spiritual rather than material; that truth and good are real and therefore evil and error are unreal; and that through prayer and spiritual comprehension, through knowing and understanding God, these facts can be spiritually achieved and demonstrated." —Wikipedia, article "Christian Science."

only the idea—and not the thing—is real, causing the church to denigrate the body ('thing') as merely a house for an eternal soul ('idea').

## To Know Truth We Must Honor the Creator Who Is Truth

To understand truth we must first recognize the Creator whose world of *real* 'things' reveals His divine mind and yet forever remains distinct from Himself. To deny either the material reality (*tangible* thing) or the spiritual reality (*intangible* idea) either reduces God to a mere power within nature (Plato) or it exalts the creature to deity (Aristotle)—as the serpent promised in the Garden.

All idolatry comes from one or the other of these misperceptions—either treating the 'idea' as a reality greater than 'things,' as in Plato, and thereby disregarding the Creator as the source of both ideas and things; or treating the creature ('thing') as the reality, as did Plato's famous pupil Aristotle, thereby disregarding God as the One who made the thing. Both Platonic and Aristotelian concepts of reality, with their contrasting languages, were absorbed by the early church. One focused on invisible/intangible ideas, the other on visible/tangible things. The dialectical combination of the two produced the Papacy.

Aristotle

Ellen White identifies the Papacy with the beast power that comes out of the "sea" in Revelation 13:1–10. Together with the beast that comes out of the "earth" of Rev. 13:11, which she identifies with Protestant America, the Papacy is soon to enforce creature worship in defiance of the three angels' call to worship the Creator and warning to not worship the Beast. In this context, she explains how the Papacy appeals to two classes which embrace nearly all of humanity who speak one or the other of the dialectical, conflicting languages that prevent integration of the poles of truth:

Popper describes Plato's concept of the soul as emerging from inner conflict and dialectic tension revealing his longing for unity. "Nowhere," he declares, "does this inner struggle reveal itself more clearly than in Plato's theory of the soul. That Plato, with his longing for unity and harmony, visualized the structure of the human soul as analogous to that of a class-divided society shows how deeply he must have suffered. Plato's greatest conflict arises from the deep impression made upon him by the example of Socrates, but his own oligarchic inclinations strove only too successfully against it" (ibid., 166).

Popper opposed dialectics but grasped neither its cause nor the unity of paradoxical truth, failing to distinguish between the Creator and His creatures.

*The Papacy is well adapted to meet the wants of all. It is prepared for two classes of mankind, embracing nearly the whole world,—those who would be saved by their [tangible, conservative human] merits, and those who would be saved in their sins [by intangible, liberal, divine grace]. Here is the secret of its power. —The Great Controversy, p. 572.*

Here she describes the results of centuries of absorption of Platonic and Aristotelian philosophies. While Aristotle's philosophy stimulates the righteousness of tangible, human works, Plato's philosophy encourages dependence upon abstract grace devoid of human effort and obedience.

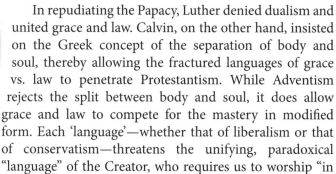

John Calvin

In repudiating the Papacy, Luther denied dualism and united grace and law. Calvin, on the other hand, insisted on the Greek concept of the separation of body and soul, thereby allowing the fractured languages of grace vs. law to penetrate Protestantism. While Adventism rejects the split between body and soul, it does allow grace and law to compete for the mastery in modified form. Each 'language'—whether that of liberalism or that of conservatism—threatens the unifying, paradoxical "language" of the Creator, who requires us to worship "in spirit and in truth" (inner motive and external behavior). Thus, the three angels' call to worship the Creator alone is a call to discard entirely the neo-Babylonian languages of the Papacy.

## Liberalism and Conservatism Both Foster Idolatry

All worship is false unless the 'thing' and its 'idea' unite in subordinate relation to the Creator. True worship requires both literal obedience and loving conceptual response to the mind and will of the Creator. By this literal/spiritual response, man voluntarily merges his will with God's will so that the two become one, though each retains its own individual reality!

Failing to respond to that which God has revealed of His will allows the blind, internal motives of liberals or conservatives to favor that side of paradoxical truth which best defends self. Dialectical thinking seldom denies the converse pole of truth; it simply subordinates and conforms it to unrecognized motives which protect "king self's" sense of security and prevent an equal "hearing" of the other pole of truth!

Thus, Conservatives, who seek security through behavioral obedience, unwittingly lean toward Aristotle's focus on tangible nature and law, undermining intangible 'ideas,' and Liberals, who seek security by imbalanced focus upon intangible 'ideas,' gain a sense of security while allowing relative freedom from obedience and the guilt that results from disobedience. Both avenues lead to idolatry which passes for true worship as each focuses unwittingly upon personal security more than upon the Creator. The purpose of the three angels' messages is to purify worship by exposing the false forms of worship that do not unite the creature to the Creator.

Giving glory to God by caring for the body, which is the temple of the Holy Spirit (called "health reform" by Seventh-day Adventists), provides a *visible* means of reflecting the *invisible*. As the heavenly temple is presided over by our High Priest, His ministry in heaven is united with the Spirit's ministry on earth. That is why Paul writes to the Romans:

> "I appeal to you therefore, brethren, by the mercies of God, to present your bodies as a living sacrifice, holy, acceptable to God, which is your spiritual worship." —Romans 12:1, RSV.

"Health reform," or caring for the body temple of the Holy Spirit, is therefore vital to spiritual worship; yet, if one's focus is not upon Christ and a humble relationship with Him by the Holy Spirit, "health reform" will tend to breed self-righteousness and legalism. The key to restoration of paradoxical reality by the third angel's message is a Spirit-directed focus on the supreme truth of the incarnate, human *and* divine Creator-Redeemer.

According to Paul, the Spirit is only free to direct us as we yield our bodies as His temples. To seek relationship with Christ without treating the earthly body as the Spirit's temple is presumptuous. On the other hand, careful attention to temperate habits without dependence on Christ results in legalism and Phariseeism. Unless both are united, neither is honored, for the ministry of the Spirit in our earthly temples depends upon the ministry of Christ in the heavenly one, and what Christ accomplishes in the heavenly is only effectual when we accept the Spirit's ministry in the earthly.

# —Chapter 10—
# Hegel Throws Away the Key

*"The dragon was wroth with the woman and went to make war with the remnant of her seed, which keep the commandments of God and have the testimony of Jesus Christ." —Revelation 12:17.*

H egel was a brilliant rising star of only 28 when, in 1798, the proclamation of Daniel's "time of the end" prophecy began. He came upon the scene just in time to use his divinely gifted mind to help unseal Daniel's sanctuary message. His fame coincided with the proclamation of the Advent message in Europe. And he died in 1831, just as the message of the Advent was being subverted by J. N. Darby and as William Miller was called to the pulpit from the plow to restore in America the historicist principles of the first angel's message which Darby had perverted.

Indeed, Hegel was in hot pursuit of truth. But like Plato, he threw away the key of knowledge. He identified the dipolar nature of truth which is to prepare the world for Christ's coming; but, instead of demonstrating its unity, he denied its Author and placed its poles in opposition to one another. Casting aside the authority of Scripture, the only sure test of reality, he denied truth by accepting the illusion of conflicting evolutionary forces which are falsely presumed to be the agent of progress.

Thus, instead of dedicating his brilliant mind to proclaiming the first angel's message, he prepared the world to reject the Creator by promoting dialectical historicism. Plato's dialecticism had already perverted the early Christian church, giving rise to the Papacy, and then it corrupted Protestantism. Hegel now imposed a permanent fracture of paradoxical truth upon the whole world. Thus, he not only denied the Creator in whom the poles of truth unite, but he threw away the key that would give others access as well.

Instead of honoring the Creator, Hegel declared all changes to be the product of opposite natural forces. A given force (thesis) arouses an antagonistic force (antithesis) which engages the first force in conflict until one subordinates the other in a new synthesis. And on and on the never-ending cycle of thesis-antithesis-synthesis goes.

Instead of two sides of a single reality, Hegel thus denied any permanent reality and proclaimed a 'split-truth' message. That message, as conveyed through Charles Lyell's evolutionary geology, sent Darwin on his famous 1831 journey on the S.S. Beagle to the Galapagos Islands at the very time William Miller began to preach. While Plato denied the reality of the 'thing' in favor of the 'idea' and Aristotle denied

Galapagos Iguana

the reality of the 'idea' in favor of the 'thing.' In a sense, Hegel denied both by his theory that 'idea' and 'thing' are in constant conflict in which they are ever becoming but never arriving. Thus, for Hegel, truth is seen to consist in neither the 'idea' nor the 'thing,' but in their ceaseless conflict as each vainly seeks to emerge triumphant as permanent reality.

## Two Universal Systems Counter the Three Angels' Call to Worship

Hegel was right in denying that either of the part-truths was truth, for neither pole is true by itself. To be true, the sphere of truth requires the unity of its hemispheres. Heresy's power lies in part-truth, with vital paradoxical elements isolated and pitted against each other.

The first angel's call to worship the Creator is a call to unite humanity with divinity. It offers the paradox of divine law and human observance of the Sabbath as a sign of loyalty and true worship of the Creator. But this message can have no meaning to one who denies the Creator and assumes that truth has no permanent reality, but evolves in ever-recurring cycles of thesis, antithesis, and synthesis!

This evolutionary weapon against the three angels' messages revolutionized history, inspired two world wars, bred half a century of "cold war," and now threatens civilization with extinction. As a counter-gospel, Hegel's dialectical "good news" is a never-ending cycle of conflict which guarantees a perpetual, evolutionary process forever eluding reality.

Hegel, like Plato, never found the meaning of truth for neither grasped the master key to the competing forces. It is a warfare between good and evil in which two supernatural beings engage in a fight to the finish for dominion of the world by control of man's mind. One of these seeks to set the mind free, the other determines to keep it enslaved.

In subverting paradoxical principles by dialectical processes, Hegel reveals the universal plight of all mankind. We begin life with minds enslaved by fractured truth because of a fractured relation between the creature and the Creator. That enslavement can be overcome only as, by the Spirit, we transcend both 'things' and 'ideas' by merging our wills with the will of the Creator.

## Divine-Human Unity of Truth: Known Only by the Spirit

Scripture provides many types, metaphors, and symbols to help us grasp the *unseen* by means of the *seen*. Even so, natural man cannot comprehend the link between the two unless aided by the Holy Spirit (1 Cor. 2:14–16). The Liberal's focus on 'ideas' can no more penetrate spiritual truth than can the Conservative's focus on 'things,' that is, on verbal elements of revelation. Both parties think they are rich while lacking the divine "eye salve" of the Spirit essential to see the reality of the other side of the truth (Rev. 3:18).

Had Hegel only viewed human reality in light of Spirit-illumined Scripture, he would have discerned the reason for cyclic conflict. He might have become an agent in preparing the world for the three angels' messages that provide the only solution to dialectical conflict. Without the Holy Spirit's guidance to true reality, humanity is left with a bewildering array of part-truths. Man's continual strife reveals his inherent conflict with the One whose mind is the source of reality. None can escape this conflict except by surrendering the mind to the Holy Spirit, who longs to unite the poles of truth and release its power!

Instead of producing an upward evolutionary spiral as claimed, dialectical conflict locks man into a "devolutionary" downward spiral of ever-changing forms of error, as paradoxical truths are split and their contrasting elements dialectically pitted against one another.

Estrangement from the Holy Spirit, who alone accurately interprets the book of nature, precludes comprehension of paradoxical truth. Not only does devious human nature protect self by enforcing separation of truth's two hemispheres, but sin's impact on nature confuses nature's testimony about the Creator. Faith's response to special revelation alone guarantees integrity in truth. Failure to submit to its authority deprives humans of the key that alone can reconcile conflicting perceptions of truth. Thus, in the first angel's message, which proclaims Biblical creationism, converse elements unite in ultimate synthesis which translates apparent diversity into eternal unity.

## Divine Revelation Threatened by Both
## Liberal and Conservative Thought

Recognizing a liberal threat to revelation by undue elevation of reason, Conservatives correctly insist that reason must submit to the objective Word. Nonetheless, while Liberals tend to impose reason over the written Word, Conservatives also threaten the authority of the written Word when they fail to humble themselves one to another and receive the Spirit of love while honoring the letter of the law.

Either way, Satan seeks to obscure the portrait of the Creator. Only He who is "the Truth" can prepare us for the final conflict between truth and error. While doctrinally presenting present truth, Conservatives are vulnerable to underlying strands in the dialectical web which the serpent systematically imposes upon the whole world in "the time of the end." His supreme effort is to ensnare those who respond to the Advent message. By systematizing his evolutionary dialectics, Satan has sought to inoculate the entire world—east and west, north and south—against the proclamation of the judgment hour of the everlasting gospel (Rev. 14:6, 7).

Indeed, his primary scheme is to capitalize on the explosion of scientific knowledge in the "time of the end" (Dan. 12:4) to give credence to the "scientific philosophy" that subverts the true knowledge of God as we near the return of Christ.[18]

---

18  That Daniel's statement, "many shall run to and fro and knowledge shall be increased" (12:4), refers to the searching and unsealing of the prophecies of Daniel and particularly relates to the increase of knowledge regarding Daniel 8:14 (which was left unexplained even for the prophet Daniel himself) does not preclude implications about the great increase of knowledge and vast expansion of travel in modern times.

# —Chapter 11—
# Collapse of Babylon's Conflicting Systems

*"And after these things I saw another angel coming down from heaven, ...
And he cried mightily, with a strong voice, saying, Babylon is fallen, is fallen."*
—Revelation 18:1, 2.

Satan's master strategy to keep men from acknowledging the Creator is to preoccupy all minds in part-truth conflict between two systems which deny the Creator. This is his only hope, for he knows that Christ's last-day message, if clearly grasped, will remove all error by unifying truth and excluding the error which inevitably attaches to fractured part-truths. Satan is concerned as God's people begin to seek the balance of truth that alone can remove our own internal conflict and set us free to proclaim the Creator's message with power. However, his anger is especially aroused as he sees his deceptive system of evolution threatened from within.

"The Babylon Tower" (P. Bruegel)
Symbol of Confusion

Key agents of evolutionary philosophy are in a panic. This is evident by the confusion of new theories that are in a frenzy to disguise the failure of science to shore up evolution. For a century and a half countless thousands of scientists have put forth intense and united efforts to confirm Darwin's theory of minute evolutionary changes over vast periods of time. Instead of finding the missing links, they have only disproved the theory and systematically removed the evidence considered to be links.

### Richard Milton's *Shattering the Myths of Darwinism*

Among the writers who have exposed this problem is Richard Milton, who wrote *Shattering the Myths of Darwinism* (1997). The subtitle of the book is significant: *The world of science faces the biggest challenge yet to one of its most basic beliefs.* Milton presents increasing evidence that there really are no such links. Among examples of false evidence is the famous chart by Henry Fairborn Osborn of the nineteenth century, with which most of us are familiar. Long presented as one of the strongest proofs of evolution, it purportedly depicts the development of the modern horse from creatures the size of a dog. Though it was discredited half a century ago, Milton notes that, as of 1997, this chart was still included as primary evidence of evolution in textbooks and in the *Encyclopaedia Britannica* (pp. 99–104).

After discussing the serious problems involved in dating the earth as billions of years old, he asks the question, "How could science have gone so wrong?" This he answers himself, "It is not science which has gone wrong, merely those scientists seeking to defend a single idea—Darwinian evolution" (Milton, p. 38).

Still espousing evolution, Milton cries out for objective and honest treatment of this issue. His preface tells of the treatment given his first edition (1992) by key scientists and publishers.

No attempt was made to refute its claims; but vigorous attempts were made to destroy his influence and that of his publisher, who dared "print a book that is "loony," "stupid," "drivel" and its author a "harmless fruitcake" who "needs psychiatric help.'" By such terms Richard Dawkins, who represents Oxford, one of Britain's most outstanding Universities, sought to destroy Milton and discredit Milton's publisher by character assassination. Significantly, two thirds of Dawkin's space was given to berating the publishers "for their irresponsibility in daring to accept a book criticizing Darwinism ..." Also significant is Dawkin's confession in the *New Statesman*, that he chose to write his review "lest the paper commission someone else who would treat it as a serious scientific treatise" (Milton, p. ix-x).

In concluding his Preface, Milton states, "To forestall any repetition of false claims like these [which he just iterated], let me make my position clear on both issues from the outset ..." He then flatly denies the charges that he no longer believes in evolution and that he believes the world is only a few thousand years old. "But," he insists, "I do not accept that there is any significant evidence that the mechanism driving that evolution is the neo-Darwinian mechanism of chance mutation coupled with natural selection" (Milton, p. xi).

While real science, involving careful observations, measurements, etc., continues to provide ever more advancing developments, the philosophical demand that its evidence be interpreted in harmony with evolutionary theories of the origin of life and age of the earth stand in the way of that advancement. An immense waste of effort is enforced by the very scientists who, in trying to prove survival of the fittest and missing link theories, actually prove them false. Yet, Darwin must be saved at all costs and however drastically his theory must be changed, for the alternative— fiat creation—is unthinkable!

## Efforts to Save the "King" Who Has No Clothes

Though continuing to repudiate the Creator, evidence they cannot deny is forcing some to develop concepts of evolution that virtually affirm a Creator. As we will see below, among these efforts to save king evolution, who, like the emperor in the story, is increasingly recognized as having no clothes on, is the theory of major leaps in the evolutionary process (such as minor changes in hox genes producing major changes in body forms) as a substitute for the minute changes they cannot find.

Indeed, a few confirmed evolutionists are constrained to recognize "Intelligent Design" (ID) in nature, while denying the validity of the Biblical history of beginnings. Despite the denial of "Intelligent Design" by the evolutionary community, the ID movement so frightens leading evolutionists that they are putting forth every effort to pass laws to prevent it from being taught in public schools.[19]

Overwhelming evidence against Darwin's "survival of the fittest" and the persistence of the missing links force even key scientists to openly admit the necessity of replacing the theory as it has been taught. Yet, many confess that they cling to Darwin because they consider creationism unthinkable! What a difference in progress there might have been and might yet be if scientists remained faithful to their basic principles and were open to obvious evidences to which they are now willingly blind!

---

19  Even many Seventh-day Adventist scientists, who do believe in God as Designer, do not openly confess ID for fear of losing all influence.

The desire to prevent discredit by the charge of religious bias is understandable; but there is risk in this position, for it splits the divine-human dimension of truth by categorizing it as either scientific or religious. It thereby ignores that all truth is based on creation and therefore always testifies of the Creator. An objective approach will not make the distinction between science and religion, but between the *actual evidence* in nature and the *interpretation of evidence* according to a worldview that has become authoritative.

On the other hand, since scientists generally do deny or at least ignore the relation between creation and the Creator, it is appropriate to demonstrate that they are unable to explain natural phenomena. In a personal letter, Paul Giem, one of our foremost defenders of creationism, declares: "ID advocates are right to force scientists who do not believe in an intervening God to defend mechanistic evolution without the crutch of discrediting short ages. Mechanistic evolution cannot actually defend itself credibly."

Some Seventh-day Adventists actually oppose the ID movement itself, yet not always because they do not believe, but because they see public ID efforts as a political movement in an attempt to impose religion that is subversive to science.

## Phillip E. Johnson's *Darwin on Trial*

Phillip E. Johnson's *Darwin on Trial* (1991) portrays a desperate attempt by scientists to find a new evolutionary paradigm. It is well known that evolutionists prove their own claims false in their very attempts to establish missing links. Presenting voluminous evidence against Darwinian claims, Johnson substantiates frank admissions of renowned scientists about the lack of any evidence for gradual evolution. Yet they cling to Darwin simply because they have not been able to develop a better evolutionary concept and consider creation of life forms to be utter "nonsense." Johnson thus protests attempts, based solely on philosophical grounds, to shore up evolution by insisting that it is not merely a theory, but a proven fact—an insistence that is totally contrary to the evidence!

Rather than acknowledge the implausibility of Darwin's theory, the evolutionary establishment are doing as the old-homiletics teachers used to instruct their students, "If your argument is weak, shout and pound on the pulpit!" As the 200th anniversary of Darwin's birth and the 150th anniversary of the publishing of his book *Origin of Species*, this year, 2009, is being celebrated as the "Year of Darwin." Even as they celebrate, however, the desperation of scientists who realize that Darwin cannot be saved is evident in a very different attempt to shore up evolution.

## Thomas Kuhn's "Paradigm Shift"

Thomas Kuhn illustrates how philosophical theory forces professedly objective scientists to manipulate and/or deny observable data when it violates their perception of reality. In his attempt to provide an alternative to Darwin, Kuhn proposes sudden, radical changes with no intervening links—and these on absolutely no scientific cause-and-effect basis! That is perilously close to acknowledging creation, and it is as dangerous to evolution as is Intelligent Design. Only the urgency of the crisis permits Kuhn's voice to be heard in the scientific community.

Kuhn's paradigm thus radically violates objective science and demonstrates how philosophy transforms objective evidence into subjective speculation. By "paradigm" he means a formula to explain complex concepts. "Paradigm shift" refers to a sudden change, not of facts, but in perception. Indeed, he identifies reality as perception; so if perceptions change, so does reality! Such is the result of dialectical thinking which prevents one from seeing the whole truth. Scientists are obliged by their evolutionary philosophy to ignore the most obvious scientific evidence when it conflicts with their evolutionary perception of reality.

Despite the need for a new paradigm, Kuhn could not have gained a hearing had he himself not adamantly denied a Creator, which is the obvious implication of his philosophy.[20]

## Fall of Babylon: Loss of Power to Impose Conflicting Languages

Growing confusion among scientists signals the divine preparation for the final crisis in the collapse of all dialectical systems. This will permit the fullness of truth to be heard and many captives to go free. Therefore, God patiently waits for us to learn to think paradoxically by uniting, rather than subordinating, converse principles. Only as we come to grips with our own blindness to truth that does not fit our perception (or "paradigm") will we ourselves be set free by the wholeness of truth (John 8:32). To take advantage of Babylon's collapsing paradigms, we must proclaim the three angels' messages with the fullness and power of balanced truth.

## Three Ways to Deny Reality: Marxism, Christian Scientism, and Capitalism

Marxism, Christian Scientism, and capitalism all illustrate refusal to unite paradoxical principles. Marxists deny the existence of anything but matter. The term itself, *dialectical materialism*, intentionally denies spiritual reality. By dialectical pitting of matter against spirit, the spiritual is made to appear material. Marxism insists that invisible spiritual realities simply reflect culturally determined imagination. Marxists thus reduce the two sides of truth to one: objective, testable, material reality, in which the highest value is wealth.

Karl Marx

Mary Baker Eddy, founder of Christian Science

Conversely, Christian Scientists deny the reality of tangible matter. While I was pastoring in Fairbanks, Alaska, a lady asked if the church could use clothing which her son, who was "away from home," would no longer need. I was concerned that he might return and need his clothes. But, carefully avoiding the reality of his having died, she assured me he would never need them.

---

20 See "Thomas Kuhn's Concept of Paradigm and Paradigm Change," Frank M. Hasel, *Journal of Adventist Theological Society*, Vol. 2, Number 2, Autumn, 1991.

Marxism and Christian Scientism are thus opposite dialectic processes. One denies spiritual (subjective) reality—holding that it is merely a stimulus-response manifestation of matter. The other denies physical (objective) reality—insisting that it is only an illusion of the mind. Both, under the influence of Hegel, arose in reaction to human oppression resulting from nineteenth century industrialism which climaxed in twentieth century capitalism.

Seeing Christianity as the cause of oppression, Marx and Engels accused Christians of using false illusions of spiritual principles to oppress laborers. Taking the opposite route, Eddy denied material needs and misery by reducing oppression to a state of mind!

Capitalism, the third dialectical system to deny reality, has nothing to say about theology but more subtly suppresses spiritual reality by inciting an obsession for material things. Marriage of materialism to scientific philosophy, which identifies reality with measurable, material things, virtually rules out the spiritual.

The collapse of the Marxist empire so shattered Communism's material paradigm that those imprisoned for half a century by its atheistic control have eagerly reached out for a spiritual paradigm. But most merely ended up with the dialectical capitalist form of materialism. This leaves them so empty that many are now again listening to communism's siren song.

Man's extremity is God's opportunity. For years we have faced our great opportunity and God has blessed, in spite of our speech defects. However, we have yet to restore the unity of truth that will permit the 'loud cry' to hungry people to come to the marriage feast of the Lamb!

# —Chapter 12—
# A World Dying for Want of a Wedding Announcement

*"Hallelujah! For the Lord God Almighty reigns. Let us rejoice and be glad and give him glory! For the wedding of the Lamb has come, and his bride has made herself ready." —Revelation 19:6, 7, NIV.*

The paradigm the world unwittingly seeks is the language of united truth, with Christ, the Source of truth, at its center. God gave us that language at Minneapolis, but we resisted it and few even yet grasp its unity. Is it not now time to discard the dialectical languages we have unwittingly borrowed from Babylon and learn to think paradoxically about the truth, keeping Christ the Creator at the center? Only thus can we prepare to proclaim the balanced message of truth in 'loud cry' power.

The world desperately waits for God's people to unite the paradoxical principles of truth in an objective physical obedience that is motivated by subjective spiritual principles—to "worship God in spirit and in truth." Until we unite the poles of truth internally we will go on violating both objective and subjective principles. By neglecting the key to truth given to us long ago but that we have never effectively grasped, we continue to betray the millions in darkness, including those set free from communism by divine providence.

Time is running out! Satan's long successful dialectical system, with one language in deadly conflict with the other, has cracked. Communism's military system fell with the Berlin wall. Scientific philosophy, which gave birth to communism and to capitalism, is now in serious disarray, and an apparently victorious capitalism teeters on the verge of collapse.

We have no time to lose! We must unite and internalize both principles of our message—in a unity of principles that the world unwittingly longs for and that alone can resolve conflicts and prevent wars. Only as we unite these principles in heart and practice by focusing upon Christ can we, with 'loud cry' power, offer true freedom to communists and hope to those bound in a disintegrating capitalism that hastens the scene prophetically portrayed by James:

*"Now listen, you rich people, weep and wail because of the misery that is coming upon you. Your wealth has rotted. … Your gold and silver are corroded. Their corrosion will testify against you and eat your flesh like fire. You have hoarded wealth in the last days. Look! The wages you failed to pay the workmen who*

*mowed your fields are crying out against you. The cries of the harvesters have reached the ears of the Lord Almighty." —James 5:1–4, NIV.*

Let us arise and fulfill our sacred commission to proclaim the Creator to a world confused by subjective philosophy that "hold[s] the truth in unrighteousness" (Rom. 1:18).

*"... they made nonsense out of logic and their empty minds were darkened. The more they called themselves philosophers, the more stupid they grew, until they exchanged the glory of the immortal God for a worthless imitation, for the image of mortal man ..." —Romans 1:21–23, JB.*

## To Speak Either Babylonian Language
## Is to Share Her Blindness

But how are learned men so deceived? In the same way we are. As they seek to "simplify" truth and relieve the tension between its converse poles by denying or subordinating the principle that interferes with their opinions and desires, they end up manipulating contrary evidence to fit their own opinions.

Romans 1 exposes the motives that result in such tailoring—such distorting—of truth to fit pre-conceptions and carnal desires. But are they guiltier than we who have greater light? Only as we discover how our own motives stimulate our 'split-truth' tendencies can we help those beguiled by a presumed scientific objectivity that can only betray reality.

In this crisis time, God offers to set dialectic 'split-truth' slaves free to worship the Creator. But to help them grasp truth's full orb, we must first escape our own part-truth thinking. We must learn to recognize and overcome motives and emotions that cause us to reduce tension between the poles of truth by denying or manipulating evidence that does not fit our perspective. Only as we learn to consistently honor apparently irreconcilable elements of God's Word can we truly honor Christ and call others to worship Him as Creator and source of all truth.

We are now witnessing the fall of Babylon in the collapse of its dialectical system. This will leave her powerless to retain God's people in bondage. But completion of that collapse will take place only when a whole message fully unites Creator and creature and sets its citizens free from part-truth cultural languages that have so long held them captive.

As we learn to consistently unite the poles of truth in by focusing upon Christ, our message will have power to unite truth in the minds of honest hearers. This alone will destroy the power that mystical Babylon wields by her part-truth languages. And setting them free to "come out of her" will precipitate her final collapse (Rev. 18:1–4; Dan. 11:44–12:1).

## Spotting Our Own Blind Spots:
## A Corporate Venture

At Minneapolis, God offered us a key to previously unrecognizable internal harmonies that permit us, ever more fully, to grasp truth as it is in Christ. This was not merely a matter of understanding. Only by uniting truth's poles can we proclaim truth as it is in Christ and as revealed in His Word! This is a corporate challenge, a challenge which our brethren in the 1880s failed to accept and that we have not yet arisen to.

Waggoner and Jones proclaimed the unity of grace and law by focusing on the One who unites grace and law in Himself. However, they failed to obey God's instruction of submitting all new truth to brethren of experience before publicly proclaiming it. They failed to glorify God by trusting Him to assure its approval and proclamation, and a spirit of independence prevented them from grasping God's deeper purpose in the message, to remove pride. Note the paradoxical balance in God's vital two-fold purpose:

*What is justification by faith? It is the work of God in **laying the glory of man in the dust**, and **doing for man that which it is not in his power to do for himself.** —TM 456.3.*

The first pole of divine purpose is *the removal of human pride.* This is essential to the second, *dependence upon divine empowerment.* Waggoner and Jones did deeply repent when reproved for failing to follow divine principles. Accepting the confession of their pride, God blessed their efforts. Yet, their violation had so aroused the disapproval of the leaders that God's purpose of their coming together in the 'priesthood of believers' to understand His Word was never realized. Neither have we yet, either leaders or laity, adequately learned to follow 'priesthood' principles in dealing with theological problems by prayerfully uniting in study.

## God Awaits Our Corporate Practice of 'Priesthood' Principles

To recognize our own blindness, we must honor both poles of truth in the context of the 'priesthood of believers,' which is the third principle of the Protestant Reformation and that which broke the back of the Papacy. By the same principle, we must collapse the power of Babylon's dialectical languages over sincere believers.

A vertical priesthood pole relates to individual freedom and responsibility. Everyone is accountable to Christ and must follow Him—no matter what others do. But a horizontal pole relates to interdependent responsibility. Christ places us in His body, the church. We cannot remain subject to Him, the Head, without subjecting ourselves to one another within the body. Neither the vertical nor the horizontal principle remains valid when exercised alone. To honor both poles of truth, we must surrender the heart to the will of God and submit our private judgment to the 'priesthood of believers.'

We are all partially blind because we have not adequately fused the two. Each sees problems in others that he cannot see in himself. Christ offers healing for our blindness and growth in knowledge and grace. But, to receive what He offers, we must unite individual study of His Word, in subjection to Him, with interdependent relations within His body, in submission to the Spirit. As we each recognize our own blind spots we will be able to serve as eyes for one another.

## Theologians and Administrators:
## Specialists and Servants of the Body

No one who chooses to remain apart from Christ's body or who exercises an independent spirit within the body can truly depend upon Christ. Scholars and non-scholars, denominational workers and the laity must all learn to hear each other. Responsibility for the purity of faith rests upon the whole body—not merely upon theologians and/or administrators and pastors or merely upon individuals or lay groups.

The exercise of the principles of the 'priesthood of believers' requires respect for each other. Each has liabilities, but each also has assets that are vital to the body. Most laymen have less factual knowledge and lack exposure to technical terms; but specialists may be blinded by the very depth of the special holes they dig. And none has time to research and analyze everything. Thus, the Lord wants to use the gifts of all—trained theologians and laymen alike—to unite His people and develop the body in truth.

Administrators and pastors do have a crucial role as coordinators and facilitators of corporate study. It is their responsibility to foster a casteless atmosphere in which all submit to the authority of divine revelation as the whole body tests concepts and wrestles through issues together.

It is easy to talk about the 'priesthood of believers,' but practicing the principles requires growing humility, commitment to Scripture, and confidence in the Holy Spirit's ability to guide the body. As the great Reformers themselves began to lose confidence in the Holy Spirit's ability to guide, they began to splinter Protestantism by violating 'priesthood' principles. As a result, the persecuted became the persecutors. To complete the stalled Reformation and prepare for the 'loud cry' of the Latter Rain and Christ's coming, we must learn what they failed to learn: to submit ourselves one to another in Him, trusting the Lord to guide His movement.

# Part 2
## Adventist Cultures in Conflict

## —Chapter 13—
# Practical Application of the Principles

*"That Christ may dwell in your hearts by faith; that ye, being rooted and grounded in love, May be able to comprehend with all saints what is the breadth, and length, and depth, and height; And to know the love of Christ, which passeth knowledge, that ye might be filled with all the fulness of God."*
*—Ephesians 3:17–19.*

In order for us to perceive three dimensions, God gave us two eyes. In order for us to perceive the direction of a sound, He gave us two ears. Many get by with only one functioning eye or ear, but most would have two if given a choice. Stereoptic sight and stereophonic hearing are definitely an advantage. What follows are examples from my personal experience of the advantages of seeing truth paradoxically.

### Into the Furrow of Northport's Need

In the spring of 1990, the pastor of the Northport district in the Upper Columbia Conference took a leave of absence from pastoral ministry. Irresolvable conflict with certain conscientious members who sought to control the church according to their narrow view caused him to question his call to ministry. Thinking my approach to issues was needed, Jere Patzer, then conference president, asked me if I would transfer to that district.

Bryce Pascoe, then the ministerial director, who had played a key role in the decision, had read my manuscripts outlining the principles of paradoxical/ 'priesthood of believers' and was aware of the practical outcomes of these principles in my previous district.

As secretary of the North Pacific Union Conference, Bryce recently declared regarding *Adventist Cultures in Conflict*:

*This work crystallizes a way of thinking that Leroy Moore has tested on the ground, allowing the Holy Spirit to bring reconciliation between people of faith. It is insightful in its analysis and historical perspective and provides a foundation for Christian growth and understanding. The implications of his conclusions call for prioritizing time in the Word so that one can think biblically and thus fulfill God's call to love Him supremely and "to love one another."*

The experiences below, which illustrate the uniting of paradoxical and 'priesthood of believers' principles, pertain to the five years of my final pastorate in Northport, just before retiring.

## When Integrity Stands in the Way

Although God's blessing was immediately seen in generally pleasant relationships in the district, Larry was utterly unable to grasp the principles I sought to convey. This was partly because I had been associated with the General Conference as Coordinator of Native Ministries and he and his family had a great distrust of church leadership.

Larry never challenged me, but for four and a half years he would shake my hand after services but always look away. Frequently after a sermon He would quote me to others as saying just the opposite of what they heard me say. But he was unpersuaded by their testimony, for he had heard me with his own ears.

I visited Larry and his wife several times with the specific purpose of trying to establish a relationship of confidence. I was candid in acknowledging that they believed I was teaching error, but I assured them that I appreciated their commitment to truth as they understood it and that it was their duty to think for themselves. I only requested opportunity to discuss the issues that bothered them so we could seek to establish a basis upon which they could trust me. Unfortunately, Larry felt so incapable of expressing his reservations that he would never discuss anything with me. Thus we got nowhere, except that our personal friendship was not strained, and I employed him to help build my house. He seemed as relaxed in this "concrete" relation as did I. Frankly, I liked and trusted Larry, and I think he knew it.

## Breakthrough

Then it happened—four and a half years after I began my pastorate there, some time after my house was built, and only months before I retired. Larry became so agitated during one of my sermons that he began to take notes. Though he was seated up front, he rushed to the back of the church at the close of the service and, as soon as I walked down the aisle to greet the people, began to challenge me in a very intense voice.

Far from distressed, I was delighted that at last he was willing to express his concerns. His first question was, "Why didn't you present [such and such]?" I responded that I did. In fact, I had spent considerable time doing so. I asked if he could wait until I had greeted the people, but he was too worked up. So I answered his questions while I shook hands.

Providentially, George Enquist, an elder and a good friend of Larry's, was standing just a little ways from him. Every time I responded to one of Larry's challenges, George very modestly nodded in agreement. By the time just the three of us remained, the steam was out of Larry's boilers. Recognizing George's support for all my answers, he declared meekly, "Pastor, I am a concrete thinker. Abstract thinking is hard for me."

## Christ Is Not Monocular

As I left the church that Sabbath in 1995, I prayed that the Lord would help me prepare a more concrete message for him. I was impressed to call Laura Schwimmer, a member of our newly formed Kettle Falls group where Larry was attending. "Could you," I asked, "lightly sketch the face of Christ and place the word *GRACE* over his left eye and the word *LAW* over his right?" On the left pupil, she was to place the word *Mediator*, on the right, the word *Judge*. Below his left eye, I had her place several Scripture references to Christ's role as Mediator; below his right eye, I had her place several texts pertaining to His role as Judge.

The next Sabbath I presented the same principles as I had presented the previous Sabbath and I used many of the same passages; only this time each member had in hand the portrait that Laura had produced for the occasion. My sermon title was "Christ is not Monocular." I simply described how Christ sees us as both Judge and Mediator *simultaneously*. As Judge, He must point out our sins and warn us to prepare for the judgment. But as He does, He looks upon us with pity, understanding, and mercy. Moreover, when we pray in faith, He, as Mediator, not only claims His righteousness on our behalf, but He assures us that He will empower us to obey and will Himself prepare us for the judgment (Phil 1:6).

Once again, as soon as the service was over, Larry left his position at the front of the church and was first to shake my hand as I came down. For the first time in four and a half years, he looked me in the eye and declared, "Pastor, that was the best sermon I have ever heard!"

Jesus, the Judge, never merely sees our sin and guilt; He looks upon us as the great physician of the soul who longs to use our very sinfulness as a means of drawing us to Himself, our sacrificial at-one-ment and Mediator of God's forgiveness and power. Not only does Christ behold us with binocular vision and recognize in every wrong deed a cry for help, but He created us with two eyes with which to behold and understand Him. Just as His two eyes provide stereoptic vision, providing depth of insight, even so will our seeing Him as both Judge and Mediator simultaneously give us a depth of understanding impossible otherwise. This view will remove the apparent conflict between faith and obedience and enable us to see only one image. With paradoxical, *stereoptic vision* we will see Jesus and His truth in "3D."

A couple of years later when I made an unplanned visit, Larry and I were invited to the same home for Sabbath dinner. As soon as we were seated together in the living room, Larry turned to me and asked, "Pastor, when are you going to come back and preach to us?"

## 'Priesthood of Believers' Principles

So what principles can we learn from the experience with Larry?

First, it is important to accept opposition as an expression of integrity in standing for truth as the opponent understands it, remembering that we are each responsible for our own convictions and that we are all faulty in our attempts to maintain integrity.

Second, it is important to know that, from where a particular person stands, integrity may require opposition since the individual may not be able to see the truth in our position, even if it is true.

Third, it is very important for those who feel compelled to oppose to communicate kindly but clearly the reasons for their opposition, and it is the duty of the one who is being opposed to listen carefully and courteously with a genuine desire to recognize any defects in view or relationships that become evident.

Fourth, it is imperative that we recognize that, like Larry, the opposition may not, at the time, be capable of responding in the correct way. Thus, the responsibility rests upon us to set an example of how to relate to someone with whom we differ.

Fifth, to maintain our own integrity, we may have to differ from others; but we must never treat them as enemies—even when they oppose us. It is always best to treat our opponents as honest, for we cannot read the heart. Indeed, Christ, who could read the heart, had many enemies, but He was enemy to none. We are counseled "to put the best possible construction upon the course of our brethren" (*RH*, April 15, 1880).

Sixth, we win people by beginning where they are, agreeing where we can, and gently moving from the point of mutual conviction in the direction of the pole of truth they are resisting because they cannot see how the two relate.

Seventh, only the Holy Spirit can remove enmity. Even if we prove our point, "a man convinced against his will is of the same opinion still." Convincing another person does not heal broken relations. Only as we humble ourselves one to another are we able to cooperate with the Spirit in the healing process.

## John Witcombe's Story

When John Witcombe arrived at the Northport church only two or three weeks after we did, Larry immediately asked him to take his Sabbath School class and present a series of studies. Indeed, with the change that would soon take place, John's influence on Larry was likely a key means by which the Holy Spirit prepared John also to respond to me. Any such breakthrough in understanding is the multi-faceted work of the Spirit.

John had been one of the founders of the Lord Our Righteousness (LOR) movement. His purpose was to get Seventh-day Adventists to leave our church and join what he believed was the Remnant Church. Shortly before his arrival, he and his wife Sharon had seen the destructive affects of LOR and had returned to the Church they had repudiated.

John and Sharon Witcombe

A few weeks after they arrived, John told me enthusiastically, "Pastor, you are giving us a theology to wrap around our experience." When I visited their home, they freely shared their LOR experience with me. To engage them in discussion of principles, I gave them a copy of my manuscript for

*Adventism in Conflict*, and asked them to critique it. All went well until they got to chapter 7, the chapter I wanted to engage them on. I was pleased when John called to declare, "Pastor, we see red flags all over the place in this chapter." I encouraged them to share with me their questions, which they did, while I took notes. I first affirmed that they were defending a very important principle and then indicated that I would like to share with them in writing how their principle related to the balancing principle which they saw as a threat because it seemed to contradict the vital principle that they espoused.

As I wrote out short Bible studies, they quickly saw the two poles of truth in every case and realized that neither could be truly understood apart from the other. They also found further healing from their former alienation from the Church, as they rejoiced in the depth of "stereoptic" truth, where two different principles merge to form a single image.

Four years later, John was called into the pastoral ministry in the Upper Columbia Conference by president Jere Patzer, who asked him to tell his story at John's first workers meeting. In that testimony, John told how the principles I shared, enabled him to maintain integrity to his own convictions, while recognizing the opposite pole of truth which he had resisted.

I used that testimony to introduce the paradoxical and 'priesthood of believers' principles in *Adventism in Conflict*. Now, after a decade and a half of ministry, John testifies how those same principles, as presented here in *Adventist Cultures in Conflict*, recently helped him develop a paper on Paul's statements in Romans 7 that have been a perplexity to many and a significant cause of conflict:

> *As I was reading through the manuscript of this book I was also preparing a presentation on the Romans 7 question—is it Paul's pre- or post-conversion experience. Applying the paradoxical principles presented in this book allowed me to see an answer that I had never seen before, an answer that speaks to the desperate need of Laodicea. The truths found in this book would take the steam out of so many of our current debates, answering the prayer of John 17.*
> *—John Witcombe, February 12, 2009.*

## Dialogue with Two Pastors

Pastor Steve Huey had responded enthusiastically at a pastors' meeting in which I had shared these principles shortly before being called to the Northport district. He had asked if I could not present them more fully. Before we could plan, I received the call to pastor right next to his district. As we got together to discuss the issues, he quickly and eagerly grasped both paradoxical and 'priesthood of believers' principles and acknowledged that his presentations had focused primarily on grace without adequately identifying law as its context.

Steve had at one time gone to the opposite extreme. As often happens, in an attempt to escape a legalistic posture, he inadvertently swing in the opposite direction. Sensing this helped him better understand the reason why one of his church members had so intensely opposed his ministry ever since his arrival a couple of years before.

Not long after, I gave a manuscript dealing with these principles to Lee Roy Holmes, a former pastor who had retired in the same district. As the three of us got together weekly to discuss these principles, both pastors came to better understand the other. Indeed, they were not far apart. Each heartily believed in law and obedience as well as in grace and faith, but neither had understood that their approach to these issues tended to stimulate conflict that related more to emphasis than to fundamental beliefs.

From the dialogue that ensued in each discussion, I formed a chapter and presented it to them at the next meeting. Unfortunately the book we intended to produce from our discussions was never written because of schedule conflicts that prevented our meeting together during the summer.

Later attempts to get together were also unsuccessful. Nonetheless, the results were that both men remained true to the initial principle that had driven them, yet each was careful to place it in the context of its balancing principle. As a result, tension in the church greatly subsided.

# Chapter 14

# Cultural Belonging vs. Faith of Jesus

*"So then faith cometh by hearing, and hearing by the word of God."*
*—Romans 10:17.*

A number of years ago I was invited to attend a national conference sponsored by a group of well-intentioned Seventh-day Adventists. The theme of the conference was *"Progressive Adventism: Oxymoron or Wave of the Future?"* This was followed later with a publication showing "some of the stimulating suggestions made at the conference as to how the Adventist heritage provides resources for the church's future . . ."[21]

The "resources" that were suggested are significant since they are now having an impact upon our church. The issue raised in the final meeting was "How can we pass on 'the faith of Jesus' to the future generation"? As "resources" were proposed at the forum for passing the faith on to the younger generation, an Adventist educator sitting beside me whispered, "Never mind how to pass on the faith. I wonder how I can retain my own!"

The question before us is, what is "the faith of Jesus" they want to pass on? Is it the Scriptural faith revealed by the One who died that we might live in communion with Him and who now ministers for us in heaven? Or is it a cultural faith in a Jesus determined rationally by authority vested in culture?

Richard Rice throws light on the nature of that faith.

## The Nature of True Progressive Faith

In his lecture, "Believing, Behaving, Belonging—Exploring a Larger View of Faith,"[22] Rice makes it clear that the faith to be passed on is a "progressive faith." He correctly insists that "progressive faith" is necessary for our time. But should not "progressive faith" mean continued pursuit and refinement of truth already discovered, rather than the repudiation of key principles of that truth in favor of more modern concepts?

---

21 The third national conference of the Association of Adventist Forums, *Spectrum*, editorial, "A Bold Precarious Faith," Vol. 20, No. 3, April 1990.

22 References to Rice in chaps. 14 and 15 are from "Believing, Behaving, Belonging—Exploring a Larger View of Faith," Spectrum, Vol. 20, No. 3, 1990, pp. 22–32.

Rice appropriately warned against a faith that overly depends on reason, but he based even this argument entirely upon reason. At no time did he refer to Scripture or identify its principles as the basis for faith. Again, he correctly urged differentiation between essentials and peripherals of faith, but, he left reason and/or impression to determine that difference! In no way did he suggest or imply authority in God's Word. Indeed, in his caution against rational dependence, he refers only to subjective freedom to "trust in God," but suggests no objective authority for that choice:

> ... even though reason can contribute to faith in important ways, faith is never the product of rational inquiry. No matter how much evidence there is, in the last analysis people are always free to decide whether or not they will trust in God. —Rice, p. 29.

Rice begins well in saying that faith is never the product of rational inquiry. Yet he stops short of identifying the true object of faith—the all-powerful Creator described in Genesis. He only says, we "are always free to decide whether or not [to] trust in God." Of the many gods people trust, the most popular in modern Christian circles is the "god" who created by means of gradual evolutionary change and not by fiat creation.[23]

This silence concerning the Creator and failure to imply authority in His Word is understandable. Indeed, it would have been embarrassing to remind hearers of authority in God's Word at a Forum celebrating its independence from the creation story of Genesis 1–3. It would have been most awkward to affirm that account, or the document written by the Creator Himself that declares a completed creation of the world and all that is in it in six days (Ex. 20:8–11).

Rice identifies two issues commonly raised by Forum participants:

> ... traditional interpretations of numerous biblical passages are now highly problematic. The accepted views among various academic disciplines concerning matters such as the origins of life and the age of the earth conflict with the way in which Christians, particularly Seventh-day Adventists, have

---

23 Even the Pope has gone on record as affirming Darwinian evolution. Just days ago, Times Online declared: "The Vatican has admitted that Charles Darwin was on the right track when he claimed that Man descended from apes.

"A leading official declared yesterday that Darwin's theory of evolution was compatible with Christian faith, and could even be traced to St Augustine and St Thomas Aquinas. 'In fact, what we mean by evolution is the world as created by God,' said Archbishop Gianfranco Ravasi, head of the Pontifical Council for Culture. The Vatican also dealt the final blow to speculation that Pope Benedict XVI might be prepared to endorse the theory of Intelligent Design, whose advocates credit a 'higher power' for the complexities of life." —Times Online, February 11, 2009, accessed Feb. 18, 2009 at <http://www.timesonline.co.uk/tol/comment/faith/article5705331.ece>

*traditionally interpreted important biblical passages like Genesis 1–3. Scholars in the natural sciences such as biology, zoology, and geology generally believe that life has existed on the earth for millions of years rather than several thousand, and that higher forms of life gradually evolved from lower ones. Scholarly approaches to other issues also exert pressure on a faith nurtured in an Adventist context. A careful exegesis of various texts in the books of Daniel and Hebrews raises questions about the biblical support for the traditional denominational position on the sanctuary. —Rice, pp. 23, 24.*

Rice does not specify his own belief. However, his comments are logically consistent with the forum hermeneutic of seeing Bible authority as relating only to spiritual issues. Though nature and Scripture are rightly claimed to harmonize since they have the same Author, scientific evidence is considered far more objective and definitive than Scripture and is logically seen as the key to harmonize the two. From this point of view, it is unreasonable to hold Scripture as authoritative over what is taken as scientific evidence.

This hermeneutic underlies Rice's claim that "a careful exegesis of . . . Daniel and Hebrews raises questions about the biblical support for" our fundamental view that Daniel 8:14 predicts the beginning of a pre-advent judgment in 1844.[24] Such questions are inevitable to those who believe that Scripture is very pliable and conclusions regarding it are to be determined by reason.

This method of interpretation and the cultural authority behind it virtually assure acceptance of the claim that our interpretation of Daniel and Hebrews is not Scriptural—despite increasing evidence that it is! Indeed, the most important issue we face is that of hermeneutics, or method of interpretation. Opposite methods yield opposite logical results. We dare not choose between these opposites; for conservative and liberal hermeneutics both tend to be imbalanced.

## In What God Do We Trust?

The session theme was significant: "Progressive Adventism: Oxymoron or Wave of the Future?" Repudiation of the historicity of Genesis 1–11 (which includes the

---

24  Scripture should be interpreted in its *natural* sense. In other words, it must be taken literally unless there is some evidence that the expressions employed are in some way figurative (i.e., symbolical, metaphorical, allegorical, etc.). The picture representations of Revelation are obviously symbols (cf. Rev. 1:1). Jesus isn't a lamb covered with eyes. Metaphors, such as trees clapping their hands, are very obvious. So are allegories, such as Mt. Sinai vs. New Jerusalem. These are not to be taken literally. Nonetheless, to classify the specific, detailed literal creation account as an allegory or merely poetic, seriously violates the principle of literal interpretation and leaves no possibility of assuring the validity of any Bible record or doctrine!

account of the flood) is indeed a wave of liberal Adventism's future; but it is an oxymoron so far as "the faith of Jesus" (Rev. 14:12) is concerned.[25]

Indeed, to deny the authenticity of Christ's own repeated affirmation of Genesis 1–3 and yet claim to believe in Him who reveals Himself from Genesis to Revelation is contrary to reason itself. One hardly reveals trust in the God of Scripture in repudiating Scripture's authority.

The fault lies not in the exercise of reason, but in establishing reason as authority for belief. The Creator gave us rational faculties to use. But He made reason subject to a higher, objective authority that tests its reliability and corrects any deviation from the revelation of His own mind.

To place our faith in culturally-bound reason is both blind and irrational, and the irrationality deprives us of the ability even to know in what god we trust. More, it denies freedom by enslaving us to impulse and impression! Genuine "trust in God" comes only by continuing in His Word (John 8:31–32). Accepting the authority of Scripture for belief and practice is the only thing that can set us free from blindness due to prejudice and dialectically-tailored truth.

## Fulfilling Our Longing for Belonging

In promoting openness to change as vital to growth in grace, Rice acknowledges the "precarious" nature of "progressive faith." We heartily agree that openness to truth is vital to spiritual growth, but openness that is not anchored in the authority of God's Word is neither progressive nor the basis for growth in grace.

Rice suggests that we reverse the generally accepted formula of *believing, behaving,* and *belonging,* and accept as our norm *belonging, behaving,* and *believing.* This reverse formula he attributes to a "Reconstructionist" Jewish rabbi whom he described as "more liberal than Reformed Judaism [which denies Old Testament authority] and more conservative in practice and observance than Conservative Judaism."

Putting *belonging* first and *believing* last actually blends Liberal and Conservative errors. It negates Scripture's authority by placing cultural Adventist *belonging* first, followed by behavior that cannot be based on faith because it is identified as a product of *belonging* that precedes faith—and faith comes by the Word (Rom. 10:17).

The *believing* that comes last is thus not faith in Christ and His Word but in the authority of culturally-determined behavior. Such believing cannot justify, for justifying faith is not determined by culture. It is only when we believe and trust

---

25  From the beginning, our faith has been located in Christ-crucified and His ministry in the heavenly sanctuary as it relates to Daniel 8:14 and its announcement of the final atonement.

fully in Him that we are justified. This is a matter of individual surrender to Christ as we receive His righteousness by faith in exchange for our sin.

Paul identifies a cultural approach as "another gospel" that is not really another, but a deception (Gal. 1:6–13). True *belonging*, as with *behaving*, rests upon a personal faith relation to Christ and His Word. It cannot be based on changeable culture that, at best, produces only legalism and an alien standard; for whatever obedience is attempted can only rest on ability to conform to that cultural norm.

*Belonging* has two belief-based dimensions: the human and the divine. The most tangible of these is the human sense of acceptance the believer has in Christian fellowship that may be closer than blood bonds. Such a closeness also involves an intangible, divine dimension—a shared faith in Christ with the sense of His loving acceptance that motivates behaviors and relationships. Only thus can our longing for *belonging* be fully satisfied.

Such a "faith *belonging*" provides the only basis for behavior that God can honor. It is a behavior that springs from the heart in obedience—a behavior legalism cannot produce.

## Paul Protests Cultural Faith

Indeed, Paul repeatedly repudiates cultural *belonging* as the basis for faith. Throughout his whole ministry he opposed cultural Judaism, though not repudiating circumcision, *per se*, for he circumcised Timothy (Acts 16:3). His opposition was to superimposing the authority of a ritually-based culture upon faith. According to Galatians, cultural Judaism is "another gospel" because it denies the centrality of faith in Christ.

The faith required is neither primarily doctrinal nor merely intellectual. It is "the faith of Jesus" (Rev. 14:12)—not simply the kind of faith He had, but His Spirit-instilled gift of faith. By this gift we confidently respond to His Word and lay hold of its power as we seek to know and to obey God's will.

The nature of faith is crucial, for if our faith is not based on God's Word in personal response to Christ, then what we claim as faith is mere presumption. The devils themselves can boast such "faith."

Laodicean faith unwittingly substitutes presumption for "the faith of Jesus." A self-satisfied sense of security, engendered by false faith, obscures the straight testimony of the True Witness, and the result is a self-righteousness that prevents exposure of the presumptuous self will.

No matter how genuine faith is, it, by itself, does not save. "There is nothing in faith that makes it our saviour" (*Reflecting Christ*, p. 78). Faith is merely the faculty by which we respond. But it can be focused either upon Christ or upon a satanic deception. We are saved by Christ through His grace, as revealed in His Word, and received by the faith it inspires (cf. Rom. 10:17). Thus, there are two factors involved, not only one. Salvation results when, by faith in His Word, we respond to Him personally as our High Priest as well as to His cross. We are saved by placing our faith in *Christ* who, in the sanctuary above, takes our sins and ministers to us His own righteousness.

## The Divine Order is *Believing, Belonging,* and *Behaving*

To give *belonging* priority over *believing* would not be so serious, though still confusing, if *belonging* meant *belonging* to Christ, rather than to Adventist culture. Yet, even that would be irrational, for spiritual *belonging*, if it is *belonging* to Him, involves the new birth and requires an act of faith in choosing to believe in Him.

The most serious of errors is placing *behaving* before *believing*, for this is a sure recipe for legalism. Acceptable *behaving* must not only be a product of faith, it must and will be a product of *belonging*. As soon as we believe in Christ, we belong to Him and are identified by Scripture as being "in Him."

The formula must therefore be *believing, belonging,* and *behaving*. As Paul repeatedly declares, we are not saved by works of obedience or behavior (Gal. 2:16; Eph. 2:7–9). Acceptable *behaving* must be firmly based upon a faith in Christ that involves *belonging* to Him and to each other as brothers and sisters in faith. If we are "in Him" by faith, we belong to each other in the fellowship of saints.

Rice, however, in no way relates *belonging* to Christ, His Spirit, or His Word. His remarks are strictly cultural, relating to a kind of *belonging* that one might have in a garden club or any other social organization—a socio-religious fellowship in Adventist culture.

This raises a question as to the validity of culture. Is culture legitimate? Or must we oppose culture itself, as some feel compelled to do? What role, if any, should culture play in our lives? And, if we should honor culture, on what basis should that be? What about the issue of authority? Culture certainly does involve authority.

# —Chapter 15—
# Does Authority Lie in Culture or the Word?

*"And God said, Let there be light: and there was light. ... And God called the light Day and the darkness he called Night. And the evening and the morning were the first day." —Genesis 1:3, 5.*

The faith of Jesus, "the Word" made flesh (John 1:1–3), cannot be separated from faith in His Word by which He created the world and by which He reveals both Himself and His principles of life. Any other faith is deceptive self-trust that produces false security! It is therefore most urgent that we believe the Genesis record of His creative activity by which, through Moses, He introduces His Word!

Four elements, in the account of each day of material creation, combine to emphasize the literal nature of the account: (1) a divine command—"God said let there be," (2) material fulfillment—"and it was so," (3) affirmation of its completion—" and it was good" and (4) a declaration of the 24-hour length of that day—"And the evening and the morning were the ___ day." Thus, the creation on each day of 24 hours came immediately and in a complete state upon divine command in instant fulfillment of the spoken Word.

## Is Belief in the Creation Story an "Adventist Version of Lysenkoism"?

In the final lecture of the series, former Forum president, Alvin Kwiram wrapped up the presentations:

*Like the Soviets, we [Adventists] have restricted the information flow and functioned defensively. We exhibit many of the characteristics of a closed society. Inevitably, such an inflexible organism will become frozen in time, like some great intellectual, wooly mammoth ...*

*An example is the Adventist version of Lysenkoism. Lysenko was a Russian agronomist who did not believe in genes or plant hormones, and insisted that environmental factors be genetically transmitted. His views dominated Soviet research and scholarship in the field of biology, and essentially ensured that Soviet scientists were totally left out of discoveries in molecular biology ...*

*In the case of Adventism, the problem is not so much biological as geological. At a time when nine out of 10 Adventist scientists reject the 6,000-year model for the age of the earth, the church still seems to take its cues from the few remaining adherents of that anachronistic view. —Spectrum, Vol. 2, Num. 3, 1990.*

"Nine out of 10" is questionable. Perhaps he was including all Adventist scientists who think gaps in the Biblical record could account for several hundred or even a few thousand extra years. Even still, it would be seriously misleading to include Adventist scientists who honor the Biblical six-day creation week with those who deny it in favor of creation by evolution. In any event, truth has never been determined by majority belief. If we cannot trust clear and explicit statements in God's Word, what part of Scripture can we trust? And what authority would we have for any of our beliefs—except that of ever-changing culture?

## To Lose the Authority of Christ and His Word is to Lose Everything

In view of the disarray of evolutionary philosophy, who are the Lysenkoists? Who are the ones who are not acknowledging the failure of their theories? Not once in the four-day Forum were any of the four factors accompanying each day of creation even alluded to, let alone affirmed. During the question-and-answer period at the close of the first plenary session, I had barely commented to my seat-mate that to deny the historicity of Genesis is to threaten every doctrine of Scripture, when a man took the microphone and denied both the incarnation and the resurrection. As a panel member he later claimed all accounts of Christ's miracles and divinity were merely allegorical.

Thus, cultural arguments for the Sabbath replace Scriptural authority. Rice states:

*The best example of what I have in mind is the fresh approach to the Sabbath many Seventh-day Adventists have taken in recent years—a development that may be traceable to a visit by Abraham Joshua Heschel to the Claremont Adventist church in the early 1960s. ... This revisionary perspective on the Sabbath, that emphasizes its potential as a resource for modern human beings, reveals that we can affirm a traditional element in Adventism in nontraditional ways and for reasons that may never have occurred to our denominational forebears. New data often make it necessary to revise traditional beliefs, but they can also give us new reasons for making time-honored affirmations. —Rice, p. 29.*

We welcome fresh efforts to show the importance of the Sabbath. Indeed, it is not only the basis for the first table of the Decalogue, but also for the second. It is a key to the gospel, an insignia of justification by faith. And even before sin, it was given as a building block for cultural development. After the fall, it is the basis for both human and divine spiritual fellowship and declared a test of faith in Him who created by His Word a state of things He declared "very good." Moreover, it is His sign of true worship in response to His call to "Fear God and give glory to Him" because He created all things pertaining to the earth in six days (Rev. 14:7; Ex. 20:11).

We lose everything if anything replaces the authority of Christ and His Word! To advocate the Sabbath but deny the Creator's own account of creation involves radical surgery in transferring the Creator's authority to the creature and its culture. The patient cannot survive such a surgery!

## Did Christ Deceive Us by Detailed Emphasis of a Literal, Six-Day Creation?

To replace Scriptural authority by cultural authority re-enacts Eve's choice to depend on her faculties of vision and reason rather than on God's direct revelation. Do we dare put greater confidence in other creatures, in our own senses, or in our reason than in God's Word?[26] Is it safe to repudiate what the Creator Himself inscribed with His finger?

*"Remember the Sabbath day to keep it holy. ... For in six days the* LORD *made heaven and earth [and] the sea ..." —Exodus 20:8,11.*

*"And he gave unto Moses, when he had made an end of communing with him upon mount Sinai, two tables of testimony, tables of stone, written with the finger of God." —Exodus 31:18.*

Did Moses deceive us by misreporting either the fact of God's own handwriting or of what He wrote? Did the Creator, divine Author of the creation account, deliberately deceive us by declaring a six-day creation week as the reason for our worship if it actually took billions of years? How can we trust Him at all if we cannot trust His self-revelation? Of what value is it to preserve and pass on such a "faith of Jesus"?

To question the integrity of the first Old Testament writer is to question the integrity of the entire Bible, including the final book which is described as "the revelation of Jesus Christ" and which contains scores of allusions to the Old Testament and a direct reference to the creation account. Notice the comparison of Exodus 20 and Revelation 14:

---

26  Note that reason or reasoning does not mean "rational." As a matter of fact, Eve's reasoning was irrational, thus against reason. But she trusted her faculties of sight and reason (seeing is believing) against revelation, which is always irrational and its consequence, sin, is insanity.

*"... in six days the L*ORD *made (a) heaven and (b) earth, the (c) sea, and (d) all that is in them, and rested the seventh day; therefore the L*ORD *blessed the Sabbath day and hallowed it." —Exodus 20:11, RSV, emphasis added.*

*"... worship him who made (a) heaven and (b) earth, the (c) sea and (d) the fountains of water." —Revelation 14:7, RSV, emphasis added.* [27]

To question the integrity of Moses, the first Old Testament writer, is to deny the authority to which Jesus repeatedly testifies, [28] as in Luke 16:31: "If they hear not Moses and the prophets neither will they be persuaded, though one rose from the dead." Upon Jesus' resurrection, He appealed to Moses as the authority for the prophetic fulfillment in His earthly, Messianic ministry (Luke 24:27).

With a six-day creation week at the heart of our message, how could "progressive faith" deny, not only Genesis 1–3, but Jesus' personal testimony while on earth, as well as the Decalogue written with God's own finger? Is the repudiation of the testimony of Jesus, Moses, and John to be considered progressive?

## Peter's Prediction Anticipates the Rise of Theistic Evolution[29]

The call for universal worship of the Creator in light of the judgment (Rev. 14:6, 7) needs to be seen in the context of Peter's prediction about "the last days." Peter identifies those whose inclinations affect their dialectic interpretation of nature. He predicts that scoffers would arise who claim to believe in creation, yet who, dialectically ignore the evidence for a six-day creation and for the flood.

*"Knowing this first, that there shall come in the last days scoffers, walking after their own lusts, And saying, Where is the promise of His coming? for since the fathers fell asleep, all things continue as they were **from the beginning of the creation**. For this they willingly are ignorant of that by the word of God, the heavens were of old, and the earth, standing out of the water and*

---

27  The same elements are also found in Psalm 146:6, the source of which is also the fourth commandment. Thus, the first angel affirms a six-day creation week as the basis for true worship.

28  Christ affirmed Moses and/or the creation account in numerous ways. He used the creation account to supersede the law of Moses and in a way to affirm the historicity of the creation account (Matt. 24:37–39; Gen. 2:21–25). Moreover, His reference to the flood in its literal context affirms its historicity (Mark 10:2–9).

29  There are now precise ways of distinguishing between various beliefs in creation by evolution. "Theistic evolution" here and elsewhere is a generalized statement simply indicating the concept that the world is billions of years old and that creation in some way came about by evolutionary processes.

*in the water: Whereby the world that then was, being overflowed with water, perished." —2 Peter 3:3-6, emphasis added.*

Peter predicts that, in the last days, professed Christians would deny Christ's coming on the basis of a view of the "creation" which denies God's speaking the world into existence and His destroying the world by the flood, and that they would by this view believe that all things will continue as they came into being. (See also verses 10–13.) This aptly describes the view of origins claimed by those who affirm theistic evolution. Yet, this view contradicts the six-day creation account, which is the basis for all references to the origin of the world. Genesis 1 says, "And God said … and it was so." Psalm 33:6, 9 says, "By the word of the LORD were the heavens made. … For He spake, and it was done; He commanded, and it stood fast." Is it reasonable to deny the Creator's record of a fiat creation and still claim to believe in the Creator?

# —Chapter 16—
# Pharisee Culture vs. Christ's Authority

*"'Men and brethren … concerning the hope and resurrection of the dead I am being judged!' And when [Paul] had said this, a dissension arose between the Pharisees and the Sadducees; … For the Sadducees say that there is no resurrection—and no angel or spirit; but the Pharisees confess both."*
*—Acts 23:6–8, NKJV.*

The ancient Pharisees prided themselves on Scriptural orthodoxy and were sharply critical of the heretical Sadducees who, while claiming to preserve the authority of true Scripture, denied authority to any but Moses' writings. So determined were they to defend orthodoxy against the Sadducees that Paul twice turned the Pharisees and Sadducees against each other by declaring he was on trial for the resurrection, thus thwarting their united attempts to put him to death.

The Pharisees confessed the great truths that the Sadducees denied, such as miracles, and especially the resurrection. So zealous were they to uphold the whole of Old Testament Scripture that they surrounded its commands by additional injunctions which they enforced on others. Yet, far from commending their faithfulness to Scripture, Christ declared of the Pharisees:

*"In vain do they worship me, teaching for doctrines the commandments of men." —Matthew 15:9.*

Within modern Adventism, denial of the authority of Christ's testimony in Exodus 20:10, 11 and Gen. 1–11, as well as that of the Spirit of prophecy, clearly reflects the Sadducee principle of limiting the divine authority of Scripture. Yet, doctrinal Adventist orthodoxy, with its higher claims to truth and virtue, often reflects what Christ treated as even more serious Scriptural violation! He reserved His sharpest rebukes for the Pharisees (Matt. 23). From that perspective, the egocentric use and rigid misuse of Scripture in defense of orthodoxy may thus be more serious than the errors of liberalism!

Those who seek to uphold Scripture would do well to humbly search their hearts, considering that Christ's rebukes of the Pharisees resemble the accusations of the Sadducees, who were ridiculing the legalistic attitudes and interpretations of the Pharisees.

Christ's rebukes of the Pharisees did not, however, justify the Sadducees in their unbelief. Yet, they do give pause to those who are prone to judge Liberals for their views and lifestyle. Liberals may be less accountable for their failings than

Conservatives—especially in light of the failure of Conservatives to reveal the truth in the Spirit of truth.

## Beware of Liberal Infidelity and Conservative Rigidity

We dare not accept liberal methods of higher criticism which subject the authority of God's Word to human reason. However, we must take seriously their concerns about the conservative approach to Bible study. With too little consideration for context and the larger weight of evidence of Scripture as a whole, Conservatives often impose pre-conceived opinions upon isolated statements and judge the sincerity of those unwilling to accept their perceptions as the meaning of the Word of God.

This tendency prompted my decision in the 1950s to deal academically with truth-splitting on both sides of the aisle, and that, in turn, led to my 1966 master's thesis and to my 1979 book *Theology in Crisis*, which demonstrates Ford's habitual dialectical splitting of truth's paradoxes. Thus, my commitment to deal with paradoxical issues was made two decades before I knew anything about Ford and over a decade before he developed his theology.[30]

Conservative Adventists will doubtless rejoice at my claim that Liberal Adventism's cultural redesign of the gospel constitutes "another gospel," that is not the gospel, but a perversion of it. Yet, any liberal Adventist who has persevered thus far, will just as surely resonate with my challenge to conservative Adventism's opposite cultural adaptation of the gospel.

## Jesus was More of a Threat to Conservative Orthodoxy Than to Liberal Infidelity

Did orthodox Pharisees crucify Christ because He was unorthodox? By no means; He shared every orthodox doctrine. Nevertheless, He posed a greater threat to them than to the heretical Sadducees, who delighted in His challenges to the

---

30 My position then and now is that conservative Adventism is also guilty of splitting truth's paradoxes by dialectical and divisive thinking that subverts the Word. Our own failure has caused the divine Watchman to permit apostasy. Thus, following my formal thesis summary and conclusions (*Theology in Crisis*), I added a final, concluding chapter, "Personal Reflections," testifying to our corporate need to examine ourselves and our methods.

Our own failure has caused the divine Watchman to permit apostasy and heresies to enter to awaken us to the task of heart-searching study and application of Scripture. The straight testimony of the faithful and True Witness to Laodicea has long called us to repentance. He has even given modern testimonies to press home His testimony, acceptance of which tests our commitment to His Word. Yet we continue to cherish our opposite, split-truth concepts which insulate us against His message.

Pharisees. He threatened the Pharisee's sense of security by His life and teachings which reproved their lack of spirituality and threatened the very basis for their religion. Indeed, the greatest sin of the Pharisees was an orthodoxy that bred security in doctrinal purity rather than in forming a relationship with God.

Of course, the Pharisees did talk about relationships. They repeatedly justified themselves by referring to their relationship to God through Abraham. One scribe readily summarized the principles of the law in terms of relationship: loving God supremely and one's fellow man as oneself. Yet for most, relationships were only theoretical, and orthodoxy became a wall separating them from God and from other men. In the absence of spiritual relations which alone make religion genuine, their focus on Scripture had produced a cultural religion based upon a fetish for ritual and orthodoxy (John 5:39).

Christ rebuked their feigned piety, declaring, "Unless your righteousness exceeds the righteousness of the scribes and Pharisees, ye shall in no case enter the kingdom of heaven" (Matt. 5:20). He sternly denied their integrity to Scripture (Matt. 15:9; John 5:39) and had no sympathy for their sense of superiority over the Sadducees, who openly reduced Scripture to a culturally-interpreted Pentateuch.[31]

Parallels to ancient cultural counterparts within both Adventist parties warn us to listen to the True Witness! Until those who uphold Scriptural authority sense the manner and extent to which they actually undermine it, they have no hope of influencing Liberals.

---

31  I generally refer primarily to liberal and conservative extremes. But, though the majority belong to neither, to some degree most of us do in various ways violate principles on both sides. Yet, despite growing apostasy and multiplying heresy, it is my testimony that we are making progress. Increasingly, ministers and laymen alike are growing in paradoxical understanding of the Word and in non-judgmental attitudes toward others.

# —Chapter 17—
# Sadducee Culture vs. Christ's Authority

*"Jesus answered and said unto [the Sadducees], 'You are mistaken, not knowing the Scriptures nor the power of God.'" —Matthew 22:29, NKJV.*

I n identifying the reason the Sadducees denied the resurrection—"not knowing the Scriptures or the power of God"—Jesus identifies the problem of their modern Adventist counterparts who deny the creation account. As was true then, so is it true now. There are many who misunderstand Scripture because of the erosion of faith in the Creator and the power of God.

As in the time of Christ, such loss of faith often results from failure of professed believers to reveal the principles they profess. Indeed, not a few Adventist Sadducees have come from the ranks of those who were once sincere but extreme Pharisees, but whose personal failure and that of their fellow Pharisees destroyed their confidence in the power, and thus the authority, of God's Word. Some of these have to be where they are in order to maintain their own integrity in facing reality as it seems evident to them. This helps explain why some Liberals are more careful about lifestyle issues than many Conservatives.

## The Adventist Liberal Self-Image Regarding Scripture

But Adventist Liberals do not think they deny creation. Indeed, as was true of the Sadducees, they not only claim to be true believers, but consider themselves the real defenders of Scripture! The fall 1989 Forum, where Scripture was never opened, was actually designed to promote a true approach to revelation. Though they rarely even referred to Scripture and never affirmed its objective authority, nevertheless they see their position as essential to any true faith in Scripture and the Creator. The Bible, they insist, is rational and must be interpreted in harmony with demonstrable fact and reason in relation to science.

Truth is truth, they urge, whether in the Bible or in nature. Properly interpreted, they rightly claim, these always agree because they have the same Author. Thus, each must be interpreted in light of the other, and any conflict between the Bible and nature inevitably results from failure to properly interpret one or the other. Since, in their thinking, testable science speaks a far more exact language, it is clear that apparent discrepancies between science and Scripture must be solved by adjusting our understanding of Scripture. That equally sincere people adamantly defend contrary positions from Scripture is proof, they claim, that Scripture is not definitive and is thus insufficient for proper understanding.

Indeed, they hold Conservatives responsible for destroying truth by dogmatic adherence to the *words* of Scripture, while failing to determine the underlying *message* of Scripture and refusing to honestly acknowledge truth they believe to be clearly written in nature. In their commitment to "truth," wherever found, Liberals see in the natural sciences a tool by which to distinguish the real message of the Bible from dogmatic assumptions. Believing that the geological record irrefutably establishes a world billions of years old, they feel compelled to harmonize Scripture with what they see as "facts" of nature, established by objective science. (See Chapters 4-8.)

## Liberals See Themselves as Defenders of Truth Itself

Shocked by such subordination of Scriptural authority to scientific philosophy, Conservatives question how Liberals can honestly claim to be true reformers who believe their approach to Scripture is essential to maintaining the integrity of faith. Conservatives point out that science itself does not speak of evolution. Whether science speaks in favor of creation or of evolution is a matter of faith and involves philosophical deductions.

Paradoxically, while Conservatives are horrified at "dishonest" liberal treatment of Scripture and doctrinal pillars, Liberals are appalled at "dishonest" conservative treatment of truth in general. Thus, as Conservatives defend the *pillars of truth*, they are met by Liberals who claim it is more important to relate honestly to *truth itself*, wherever found, including nature.

To remove erroneous methods and attitudes of both, the urgent need is not for compromise, but for fusion of the elements of truth in both views. Only by this "stereoptic" view of the truth can we perceive its height, depth, and breadth. But this requires better understanding of the nature of truth, which Liberals insist upon, but principles of which they themselves do not grasp; nor can they while denying the authority for truth. Conversely, Conservatives frequently undermine divine authority by their rigid use of Scripture, violating its paradoxical principles!

The primary issue is hermeneutical, that is, how Scripture is interpreted. Liberals seek to correct a conservative problem which they identify as an overstressing of the *words* of Scripture (through the use of proof texts) to the detriment of its *message*. Though Conservatives generally claim to believe in message or thought inspiration, in actual practice many do reveal a verbal inspiration mentality.

Liberals, by contrast, put their confidence in what they can observe and understand, interpreting Scripture in light of science and reason.

## Liberal Confidence in their Ability to
## Interpret the Bible by Nature

Liberals are right in seeking to reconcile nature and Scripture. But they err in placing too much confidence in human ability to interpret nature. They fail to see that it is not really the facts that are speaking, but interpretations which are taken for truth that presume to tailor-make Scripture to scientific philosophy.

In viewing the Word through the filter of scientific philosophy, Liberals betray the legitimacy of their concern over failure of Conservatives to distinguish the truth of Scripture from their own opinions of it. Virtually denying the subjectivity of their own culture-driven perceptions, they take their opinions or those of the experts as irrefutable, objective "facts," while they see the statements of Scripture as culturally-influenced opinions![32]

It is difficult to understand how Liberals can be so certain about the views of the scientific establishment when hard-core evolution is in serious disarray. We have seen that the problem is so serious that some confirmed evolutionists now no longer claim very small changes over a vast period of time. After a century and a half, these are nowhere demonstrable. Trying to honor scientific findings, but refusing to acknowledge a Creator, some even suggest sudden, major leaps with no rational or scientific evidence. Others, refusing to deny the overwhelming evidences of a designer, acknowledge a design, but deny the God of Genesis 1–3 as the Designer.

Not only is scientific theory culture-driven, but Adventist Liberals, though continuing to insist on a Creator, are controlled by a sub-culture that surrenders to general (but not specific) claims of atheistic scientific philosophy. Their testing of Scripture by science and correcting it according to human reason reveals the sure result of cultural Adventism. For, if authority lies not in Scripture, it must lie elsewhere—and that elsewhere is culturally-controlled, scientific philosophy.

As a social being, man cannot exercise his reason independently of the group of which he is a part without having a different authority. That the social group serves as authority is testified to by the repudiation of evidence for design in creation.

Some Adventist scientists believe in a Creator, yet share the atheistic scientists' disrespect for those who promote evidence for Intelligent Design (ID). For this attitude they gain no respect from atheistic culture which sees any acknowledgement of the God of the Bible as a compromising of evolutionary principles, whose assumptions have been married to scientific philosophy, their real authority.

---

32  The only safe plan is to trust God's own testimony in Scripture above their interpretation of nature. Unfortunately in the Liberal vs. Conservative conflict, both sides deal dialectically rather than paradoxically with the divine-human nature of revelation— which deserves more attention than can be given here.

## Fall of Babylon Means Loss of Power
## over the Minds of God's People

As the first angel calls for universal worship of the Creator and as the world rejects that call, despite accumulating evidence in support of it, the second angel announces the fall of Babylon. The essence of Babylon's nearly universal government is rejection of divine authority. Indeed, from the tower of Babel, Babylon's system has been characterized by rejection of the Creator and repudiation of His authority. Babylon's values are always determined on the basis of rationalization controlled by societal mores. Only the wisdom and power of the Word make it possible to escape the authority of Babylonian culture.

Indeed, the first angel's message is designed to counteract theistic evolution which Peter predicted would involve a claim of believing in the Creator, while denying the six-day creation week (2 Pet. 3:3–7). The second and third angels' messages demand separation from the culture-controlled religion of Babylon, with its beast power and fast-growing image (Rev. 14:8–11).

Whatever the appearance, there are only two options: worship the Creator with faith in Him and His Word or worship culture and surrender to its control. Only in response to God's authority can we receive "the faith of Jesus" and be empowered to obey Him in the final conflict (Rev. 13:11–14:12).

As we have seen, the choice between culture and the Word poses a challenge to Adventist Conservatives as well as to Liberals. *Both* Adventist cultures are capable of threatening the authority of Christ and of His Word.

# —Chapter 18—

# Christbold and Culture: The Great Paradox

*"For God so loved the world that He gave His only begotten Son, that whoever believes in Him should not perish but have everlasting life." —John 3:16, NKJV.*

*"Do not love the world or the things in the world. If anyone loves the world, the love of the Father is not in him." —1 John 2:15, NKJV.*

*"Jesus answered, … 'Most assuredly, I say to you, unless one is born again, he cannot see the kingdom of God.'" —John 3:3, NKJV.*

Scriptural paradoxes confront us on every hand for truth is itself paradoxical. God loves the world, and receiving His love is revealed by our love for that same world. Yet, John declares that "if anyone loves the world, the love of the Father is not in him"!

The paradox lies in what is meant by "the world" and thus the object of our love. We are to love the people, whom God loves and for whom Christ died, but we are to hate the death-dealing, self-centered system of the world that nailed Him to the cross. Thus, the warning against the love of the world relates to the spirit or culture of the world—its sinful habits, customs, attitudes, and carnal desires. Jesus prayed, not that His disciples be taken out of the world, but that they be kept from its evil (John 17:15). His prayer was that we be protected from the degeneracies of human culture. John declares that, when a person loves the world's culture, "the love of the Father is not in him."

## Is Culture of Itself Evil?

Every culture of the world reveals the influence of the evil one. Every human culture perpetuates the world's principles of government from generation to generation, the common link being the self-centered principles symbolized by Babylon.

But, is all culture then evil? To consider all culture evil, *per se*, is to ignore a vital truth: God created us for culture. Nonetheless, through deception, Satan seized control of culture. Even now Christ is seeking to reestablish His authority over culture that Satan usurped. The issue is not culture itself, but whether we allow culture to be our ultimate authority.

Satan controls culture by splitting truth's hemispheres, causing some to focus on one pole and others to focus on the opposite. It matters little to him how much truth we have, if only he can prevent us from keeping the whole truth in biblical perspective, which alone can empower us and keep us integrated and whole. The evil of culture is that it splits truth and enforces one side or the other of truth, not only preventing a balance of the truth, but also causing conflict.

## Culture Is Part of the Divine Creation

Culture itself is thus divinely ordained by a Creator who placed within our very nature the need for intimate and harmonious social relations. The One who declared, "It is not good for man to be alone" (Gen. 2:18) and commanded multiplication of mankind to "fill the earth" (Gen. 1:28), designed that we belong to each other in social unity. The principle of love itself demands such relations.

Indeed, loving relations were central to creation and are central to redemption. Each individual was meant to influence all and be influenced by all. Social unity and harmony are thus God's plan. But sin alienates from God's kingdom of love and causes the divinely ordained, culture-producing social instincts to become self-centered. *It is these selfish social instincts that produce conflicting cultures.* Satan seeks to cause every member of mankind to engage in defense of himself and of his culture against any other culture. He employs his greatest efforts to maintain each in alienation from God's kingdom of love and from each other by fomenting alienation in the basic unit of society and culture—the home.

The substitution of selfishness for love is what perverts culture, and it is the means by which Satan produces continual animosities and wars. That dialectical cultural system known in Scripture as "Babylon" enslaves all mankind to its *cultures of pride* and *language of conflict.*

## Why Should We Not Develop an Adventist Culture?

Culture is by nature conservative. It functions not only to nurture, but to preserve the knowledge, principles, and values of the past, providing for the stability of society. Were it not for sin, values and concepts of truth in every generation would pass on culturally for all eternity, enriching and benefiting all. In a sinless environment that would have united the whole race in love.

So what then is wrong with fostering cultural Adventism? Was not the Forum correct in seeking to preserve Adventist culture? Should this not be our objective? The problem is not in the nurturing, preserving function of culture. The problem is in its direction and director—it is either Christ or "the god of this world." Christ's declaration, "you must be born again" "... of the Spirit" (John 3:7, 5) relates to all mankind, including Adventists. It is not an Adventist culture that we should therefore cultivate, but a culture of the Spirit. The Spirit alone inducts us into God's government of truth, centered in His love, which can be enjoyed only as it is shared. The Spirit produces a culture of truth characterized by love, through which He will proclaim God's last-day message to the world.

## Necessity of Enmity Between the Spirit and Human Cultures

Because we are carnal by nature, every human culture reflects and fosters a range of carnal behavioral patterns. Since all mankind is corrupt by nature (Rom. 3:9–22), no child is born with a spiritual nature—even if born into a devout and spiritual Adventist home. Thus, one born into a conservative Adventist home—with the highest spiritual standards—is by nature alienated from Christ's government, and must be born again—just as one born into an un-Christian home must do. This is why, no matter what standards are culturally dictated, children can only inherit that Laodicean disease whose symptoms reveal cultural rather than spiritual Christianity (Rev. 3:17). The only escape is in being born again.

So culture is not to blame and is not in itself bad. But true Christianity requires dying to self and to the self-centered principles of every earthly culture, to find new life in the Spirit. We must, by new birth, transfer into a new and heavenly culture, whose principles are at enmity—in perpetual conflict—with every earthly culture, including *both* liberal and conservative Adventist cultures!

This enmity was announced in God's first promise to man, "I will put enmity between you [Satan] and the woman" (Gen. 3:15). So long as humans possess a carnal nature and are in a world controlled by the false "god of this world," there is and must be constant conflict between the Spirit and the worldly elements of every culture (Gal. 5:17). This is true, even if it be the most balanced Adventist culture! And it remains true even after we are born again, for we retain a carnal nature which unceasingly seeks control, in opposition to the Spirit.

The new birth, requires death to the authority of self, which instinctively enforces its own particular earthly culture—a death and new birth that come only through the grace of God and the transforming power of the Word, which is available only by faith:

> "Being born again, not of corruptible seed, but of incorruptible, by the word of God, which liveth and abideth forever." —1 Peter 1:23.

Whether liberal or conservative, cultural Adventism can only perpetuate Laodicean captivity to the flesh. It blocks the signals of the True Witness who, by means of the very degeneration of Adventist cultures, earnestly warns us to repent and to be daily rescued from our own devious nature and from our culture and subculture—whatever it may be.

## Only the Spirit-Directed Word Can Free Us
## from Babylon's Cultural Bondage

Only the Word and its divine Interpreter can rescue us from the authority of the "world" and its cultures. In this way only can we remain within our culture with the power to stand free from its control. And this is what will enrage Babylon and ignite the battle of Armageddon!

There is, however, a difference between the "words" of Scripture and the "Word of God." All true worship is in Spirit *as well as* in truth. Unless directed by the Holy Spirit, we may read the Bible's words without hearing the "Word," and thus not worship Christ, "the Word." Spiritual things are spiritually discerned. Only in the process of hearing the Word are we healed and set free from the world's inner chains that enforce cultural bondage upon us. The phrase "in spirit and truth" means that, while the Bible is our textbook, the Holy Spirit is our Teacher. No matter how we may study, we can never progress beyond the elementary rudiments unless we study the Bible under the direct guidance of the heaven-sent Teacher.

Only as we truly "hear" the Word does Scripture become "profitable for doctrine, for reproof, for correction, for instruction in righteousness" (2 Tim 3:16). "Faith cometh by hearing; and hearing by the word of God" (Rom. 10:17). That we do not yet really hear the plaintive voice of the True Witness points up the seriousness of our tendency (for Conservatives as well as for Liberals) of turning down our spiritual "hearing aids" when the Spirit seeks to correct and instruct in true righteousness. Our problem is that we can only receive such righteousness as we die to self and to the authority of either a worldly culture or an imbalanced religious culture.

Whether Conservative or Liberal, we must diligently seek escape from the authority of our peculiar brand of Adventist culture. We must learn how to die daily to self and its cultural stimulators. Only thus can we live in the culture of heaven and prepare for translation.

When we are thus inclined, the Spirit will draw us out of cultural prison houses into the light of the gospel of Christ. Under His direction, we will find ourselves uniting in a new culture and a new language of whole truth—a truth that will make us free (John 8:32). This is the secret of the 'loud cry.' For this unity in truth we should pray—as we seek the outpouring of the Latter Rain!

# —Chapter 19—
## Culture's Enmity Against Divine Authority

*"Where do wars and fights come from among you? Do they not come from your desires for pleasure that war in your members? ... Do you not know that friendship with the world is enmity with God?" —James 4:1, 4, NKJV.*

*"Because the **carnal mind is enmity against God**; for it is not subject to the law of God, nor indeed can be. ... Therefore, brethren, we are debtors—not to the flesh, to live according to the flesh. For if you live according to the flesh you will die; but if by the Spirit you put to death the deeds of the body, you will live." —Romans 8:7, 12, 13, NKJV, emphasis added.*

None should try to escape *from* culture itself. Becoming a hermit can only block the Spirit's purpose to discipline and train us to reflect Christ's character by loving responses to all, whatever their attitude or actions toward us. But we must escape culture's *authority* over us by self-centered impulses which the god of this world imposes upon all. Herein is our only hope of escaping division and attaining the unity that will prepare us for heaven's self-sacrificing culture, for which Christ prayed (John 17:21–23).

### Self-Infatuated, Self-Protecting

Every earthly culture is infatuated with its own superiority. Thus, every earthly culture fosters Laodicean self-satisfaction. Moreover, every earthly culture bears seeds of hostility to all competing cultures. Since the self-renouncing culture of heaven is a threat to the pride and selfishness of all cultures, it is therefore the special object of universal satanic attack.

Numerous cultures have appeared to be Christianized. The whole Roman world took on Christ's name. But no earthly culture ever truly surrendered or ever will surrender to Him. For the flesh with its many cultural expressions "*is* enmity against God." Were it merely "at enmity" it might be healed. But since it is itself enmity, self (fleshly impulses) must die. Any apparent surrender is merely a guise for allowing the carnal nature to penetrate Christianity.

Paul clearly identifies the cause of this undying enmity, "For [the carnal mind] is not subject to the law of God, neither indeed can be" (Rom. 8:7). Self cannot surrender self; for its deepest obsession is to maintain its own independence. Self will pay any price to continue its resistance against God's self-sacrificing culture and keep from surrendering to His law of love. And that price includes extreme efforts at super-obedience.

## Love's Enmity Against Pride and Selfishness

Since every culture is the social product of various selves joined for protection, comfort, and support, each culture reflects the corporate self-centered drive of its people. We must therefore forever reject the authority of every human culture. To this end God places enmity within each heart (Gen. 3:15), the enmity of love against selfishness. This enmity demands repudiation of the authority of all self-centered cultures of the god of this world, even of self-centered Adventist cultures. Our commitment must ever be to the principles of heaven's culture of self-sacrificing love.

Despite universal perversions, all cultures also have much that is good. However imbalanced, all cultures are formed to meet human needs. In negating their false principles we must focus upon the needs that culture, however erroneously, seeks to meet. As we meet those needs in practical ways in harmony with the purpose of the Creator, we become agents of the Spirit in His plan to release deceived captives from the false answers imposed by culture.

To help people realize that God will accept them as they are, we must accept them as they are. If we want others to understand the value God places on them, we must express that value. Since all men unwittingly identify themselves in terms of their culture, we must treat all cultures respectfully—even as we deny their authority.

Our role is not to seek to destroy the influence of culture over a given group, for culture is a God-ordained function. The influence of culture was to operate under the direction of the Holy Spirit. However, because of Adam's sin, it now instinctively operates under the authority of the god of this world. Our calling is to choose the Word of God as the final authority in testing the validity of cultural mores and correcting their perversions.

## Which Authority?

The issue is clearly authority. In every human culture, the flesh in some ways resists the authority of Christ and His Word, even when it gives the appearance of being submitted to it. To meet the mind of God requires perpetual conflict with self and culture. That conflict is between the self-sacrificing love Christ gives and the selfishness and pride that lodge within culture because it reigns within self.

Unless reason, impulse, and culture are subjected to the authority of God's Word, we remain carnal children of this world, experiencing its animosities toward any who pose a threat to self. In particular, we remain in instinctive but usually unrecognized enmity toward principles of self-renouncing love. And the most subtle and unrecognized form of animosity is religious.

Liberal vs. conservative resentment toward each other reveals mutual surrender to self-centered culture. For a century we remained reasonably united doctrinally because most Adventists were conservative. But since we did not discern the 'straight testimony' of the voice of the True Witness to Laodicea, God has mercifully permitted dialectical splintering to draw our attention to principles we failed to discern. He seeks thus to arouse us to turn up our "hearing aids" and listen more carefully.

When we fail to see the hand of providence in permitting conflict to disrupt our self-security, our natural and cultural reaction is to blame one another for the fracture of our unity, as we, in self-defense, seek to retain our own sense of security. Our problem is not the other party, but a dominance of self and cultures that are increasingly revealed in apostasy, heresy, and fanaticism. As these now spring up everywhere, on the right as also upon the left, our need is to turn our eyes upon Jesus, so that He can pour out His Spirit upon us. As we permit Him to balance and empower our lives, He will empower our proclamation even as He prepares us for the 'loud cry' of the Latter Rain.

But Conservatives must first come to grips with the reason God has not yet answered their prayers for the Latter Rain. Why has He instead permitted the Church to become so splintered? In seeking to conserve God's Word and its authority, we have not recognized our real enemy. That enemy is not liberalism; it is our own bondage to self and thus captivity to our own, conservative Adventist culture. That bondage precipitated the Minneapolis conflict and continues to enforce our culture war.

*Only the supreme authority and creative power of the Word, working through the Spirit, can heal our internal conflicts.* Only He can bring an end to our divisions, freeing us to defy both self and our own culture wherever it conflicts with the principles of self-sacrificing love.

## Distinguishing Our Own Impulses from the Spirit's Voice

Our greatest challenge is to consistently distinguish our own impulses from the Spirit's promptings. Far greater than we know is our need to grasp when and how the Word collides with the mores of our own brand of Adventist culture! Such spiritual discernment awaits careful, paradoxical approach to truth that exposes habits of protecting self and its Adventist sub-culture. And this hinges upon determined effort to die to self and remain surrendered to the Word.

But, considering itself comparatively faithful, each party resists humbling of self. Unfortunately, as members of either culture begin to sense their spiritual needs, there is danger that they will compound an already serious problem. While Liberals may feel compelled to make increasing efforts to fight obedience as legalism, Conservatives, instead of sensing their own imbalance, may intensify an already too intense letter-of-the-law focus and become even more compulsive regarding behavior. The result can only be spiraling conflict, as each is repulsed by the dialectical (*one-sided*) approach of the other. And neither submits to be guided by the Spirit of truth, by whom alone all doctrine is put in proper perspective and practiced with the right spirit.

Seeking to counter Conservatives, Liberals insist that Ellen White's writings are non-canonical and bear no authority. Some even see them as the cause of legalistic imbalance. Many flaunt clear counsel regarding standards, but this is not always merely to satisfy carnal desires. Some have as great a burden for the right as Conservatives and think it their duty to expose conservative standards as culture-bound. Since they reject conservative culture as irrelevant and the cause of legalistic violation of the spirit of the Word, Liberals feel compelled to combat it.

As each side feels compelled to invest its energies in opposing the other, instead of seeking truth in the spirit of truth, our conflicting imbalanced Adventist cultures foment a culture war that makes the truth of God's testimonies of none effect.

## Key Issue: Proper Unity of Divine and Human in Revelation

The solar plexus of the conservative/liberal dispute is the source and nature of authority. Conservatives acknowledge that some elements in the Spirit of prophecy and the Bible relate to cultural issues that are no longer relevant. But, in practice, there is often failure to properly distinguish cultural or circumstantial factors from divinely revealed principles. Thus, many compulsively but unwittingly seek to preserve the culture of the past itself, rather than the valid principles that governed the past and that must now govern the present, though in a different context.

By contrast, Liberals think they honor God's Word, but culture-bound reasoning virtually denies its divine authority. Thus, cultural factors affecting the prophet and/ or those addressed are emphasized in a way to circumvent the principles, whether in the Bible or Spirit of prophecy. Such elevation of reason over revelation makes its testimony of no effect.

Conservatives may also make the testimony of God's Word of none effect in an opposite way, often by over-literalizing. We may so fear the consequent humanistic denial of divine authority that, though theoretically recognizing the human element in revelation (because Ellen White says so), we remain virtually blind to it. Thus, we may attribute divine authority to expressions that relate to cultural circumstances, such as Paul's forbidding of women to speak in church (1 Cor. 14:34, 35). In such attempts to enforce expressions relating to changing culture, we confuse the issue and direct attention away from the unchanging principles involved.[33]

---

33　Even in our own lifetime, changes in culture may make a difference in how to apply principles. For example, in the 1960s, beards and hair were a symbol of rebellion and

What keeps us from discerning God's principles in the human expression is the unarticulated suspicion that to look at the larger view will deprive us of valuable ammunition against the "other side." Yet, unless we honestly face the complex unity of infallible divine principles and fallible human expressions in revelation we will never clearly distinguish the Spirit's voice from our own thoughts and impulses.

Failure to properly unite these is both the cause and the effect of our failure to respond to the Faithful and True Witness who has long indicted us for self-righteousness. Only as we take this challenge seriously and humbly can we receive the answer to Christ's prayer for unity. And this alone will permit Him to release the Latter Rain showers!

Until the *spirit* of the law controls Conservatives' application of the *letter*, they will remain a stumbling block to Liberals, for they will misrepresent the law and insulate Liberals against the spirit of obedience. And until Liberals treat the letter of the law with deeper respect and commitment, they can never grasp the reality of principles of the Word which they think they defend. Spiritual things are only spiritually discerned (1 Cor. 2:14–16), and the Holy Spirit is not free to guide into truth those who despise "the letter" of that which He is the divine Author.

---

were rightfully frowned upon. There was nothing wrong with beards, but it was a culture factor, and growing one violated principles of witness and directed attention to self.

# —Chapter 20—
# Worship in Spirit and Truth

*"You worship what you do not know. ... But the hour is coming, and now is, when the true worshipers will worship the Father in spirit and truth, for the Father is seeking such to worship Him." —John 4:22, 23, NKJV.*

*"The fact that there is no controversy or agitation among God's people should not be regarded as conclusive evidence that they are holding fast to sound doctrine. There is reason to fear that they may not be clearly discriminating between truth and error. When no new questions are started by investigation of the Scriptures, when no difference of opinion arises which will set men to searching the Bible for themselves to make sure that they have the truth, there will be many now, as in ancient times, who will hold to tradition and worship they know not what. ...*

*... there are many in the church who take it for granted that they understand what they believe; but, until controversy arises, they do not know their own weakness. ... God will arouse His people; if other means fail, heresies will come in among them, which will sift them, separating the chaff from the wheat." —Testimonies for the Church, vol. 5, p. 707 (1889).*

This warning of heresy soon after the Minneapolis crisis is but one of several post–1888 warnings that to treat light as darkness prepares us to treat darkness as light. Indeed, the resistance of light at Minneapolis was soon followed by five major heresies.[34]

### God Permits Heresies to Arouse Us

Until recently we have tended to rest in the security of seemingly unassailable doctrines. But our very attempt to implement the 'loud cry' by intense doctrinal focus has precipitated a revolt against the consequent void of spiritual meaning in repudiation of the doctrines themselves which they identify with that void.

---

34  These heresies include: (a) projecting Daniel's time prophecies into the future, which Ellen White strongly protested—a heresy she declared she had to meet from the beginning; (b) the Indiana "holy flesh" movement; (c) Kellogg/Waggoner pantheism; (d) Jones's concept of the Holy Spirit which repudiated organization; and (e) Ballenger's repudiation of our sanctuary message.

This reaction to a dialectic focus on the letter spiritualizes truth in a way to invalidate the letter. Heaven-authenticated doctrines thus come into question because, in circumventing truth's call for death to self, we obscure truth itself. In the ensuing battle, Conservatives may appear to be in the right for they defend the authority of the Word. But the straight testimony to Laodicea indicates that unless God's authority is internalized, external observance becomes but another form of idolatry—another way to worship the creature!

Imbalanced focus upon behavior undermines God's Word as surely as did Judaism. The law of the Spirit does not, however, diminish the importance of the letter of the law and behavior. Liberals are lost in a maze of rationalism, not because they seek deeper meaning; but because they fail to consider that to internalize spiritual realities, literal elements must be carefully cherished and their principles faithfully observed. The validity of our 'ideas' depends upon the integrity of 'things' (letters, doctrines, practices, etc.) which point to them. To diminish either doctrine or practice is thus to debase internal experience and separate from the divine Revealer!

But to hold Liberals responsible for our dilemma because they diminish the letter in the name of the Spirit and elevate reason over revelation is to prevent heresy from doing its divinely permitted, purifying work. For God permits heresies to arouse us to the heart searching that is essential to purification which we find difficult to experience.

We do well to consider the nature of heresy, as it relates to truth, and the manner of its appeal. To deceive, Satan has to depend upon truth. Garments of truth are thus stolen to hide features of heresy.

## Whole Truth Casts Out Error

But truth, when whole, exposes and thrusts out all error. Hence, to succeed, Satan must cause us to split truth's paradoxical sphere into its contrasting hemispheres and impose upon them mutually antagonistic languages (dialectics). To prevent recognition of this he gets each hemisphere to defend its truth against the other, thus causing both sides to become blind to truth's correcting power.

By magnifying differences between objective and subjective elements, Satan turns each so it cannot fit the other; thus he enforces conflict that distorts both elements of truth. Since all true principles are paradoxical, every part is divisible into apparently contradictory hemispheres. And since minds inevitably seek to defend and exalt self, we are all naturally attracted by dialectic thinking that affirms our own opinion. In this way he removes truth's corrective power.

Each side appears to its proponents to represent *the truth*. But both part-truths enforce creature worship in the guise of Creator worship. The great issue is to understand the True Witness's denunciation of creature worship and learn true loyalty to the Creator by embracing both poles of His truth. Only in openness to full disclosure of truth regarding ourselves can we distinguish between true and false worship. Without this we can never adequately grasp the indictment through the 'straight testimony' of self-righteousness which leads us to assume we are right and the other person is wrong (Rev. 3:14–17).

## Resistance to Straight Testimony Confuses Witness

Despite much defeat and limited victory in our Christian experience, our Laodicean senses deceptively assure us of our rightness, even as He seeks to correct us. Unrecognized conservative resistance to the authority of his diagnosis and prescription (Rev. 3:18–22) confuses our witness. This is why our proclamation, "Babylon is fallen … Come out of her," remains without 'loud cry' power to release her captives. Both Conservatives and Liberals need a clearer understanding of the nature of true worship for it is at the very heart of our message. Said the first angel, "Fear God … and worship Him" (Rev. 14:7).

The pillars of our faith form a vital bulwark against error. But doctrines themselves can no longer hold back the tide of heresy now threatening to overwhelm us—not merely liberal heresies but, increasingly, conservative heresies. If the spirit and the letter of the law are not united, doctrines that appear so sure may suddenly leap away from us like lightning. For the inner soul that is left unfed cries out for the spiritual meaning that suddenly appears to be offered by a spirit which seems to be from God but is divorced from His law.

Three factors now combine to make the false religious revivals sweeping the Christian world increasingly attractive as a presumed key to our dilemma: (a) a sense that we must somehow induce the long awaited 'loud cry'; (b) recognition of our weakness and deadness, and our comparing of this to a lively and powerful charismatic movement; and (c) despite doctrinal differences, an inner cultural harmony with Evangelicals, who appear to have the power of the Spirit we have long looked for, but who resist God's law and sanctuary message.

# —Chapter 21—
# Minneapolis and Celebration Worship

*"O sing unto the* LORD *a new song; for he hath done marvelous things: … Make a joyful noise unto the* LORD, *all the earth: make a loud noise, and rejoice, and sing praise. Sing unto the* LORD *with harp; … [and] with trumpets and sound of cornet …" —Psalm 98:1, 4-6.*

Responses to celebration worship, a relatively new phenomenon within Adventism, are strong but mixed. Some see in it hope; in others it arouses grave concern. Thus, it has markedly intensified our division. Most responses on both sides of the question bear earmarks of dialectical thinking, with *a priori* convictions ruling out careful, fair examination. The issue has raged for over two decades, though enthusiasm for its use has been dampened by the departure from the denomination of a number of congregations with their repudiation of the pillars of our faith—including the Sabbath.

The primary argument for its promotion is the need to reclaim and/or hold our young people by offering them escape from what they see as meaningless formalism. Some see in celebration worship a key to the pouring out of God's Spirit. Others intensely oppose it as inviting a false Spirit. Two concerns are dominant, one relates to attempts to stimulate emotions, especially by music, and the other relates to setting aside standards and replacing Bible teaching with music, drama, etc.

There is also a feeling that celebration is contrary to the solemnity of the judgment hour message. Yet, the call to celebration in Psalm 96 is cast in the context of the future judgment—a judgment which has special pertinence to God's people in this present judgment hour:

*Oh, sing to the* LORD ***a new song!*** *Sing to the* LORD, *all the earth. Proclaim the good news of His salvation from day to day. Declare His glory among the nations, His wonders among all people. For the Lord is great, and greatly to be praised: He is to be feared above all gods. For all the gods of the nations are idols: but the Lord made the heavens. Honor and majesty are before Him. Strength and beauty are in His sanctuary. Give to the Lord, O kindreds of the peoples,* ***Give to the Lord.*** *… the* ***glory*** *due His name; … Say among the nations, The Lord reigns. …* ***He shall judge*** *the peoples righteously. Let the heavens rejoice, and let the earth be glad. … For, He is coming. … He shall judge the world with righteousness and the peoples with His truth. —Psalm 96:1-8, 10, 11, 13, NKJV, emphasis added.*

## The First Angel Calls for Appropriate Celebration Worship

To object to celebration worship on the basis of the solemn judgment thus hardly seems valid. Not only does the celebration called for by the psalmist relate specifically to the judgment, but the first angel's message summarizes that Psalm in light of present judgment! The "new song" that introduces it testifies to final victory over the beast.

*And I heard the sound of harpists playing their harps. They sang as it were a* **new song** *before the throne. ... Then I saw another angel flying in the midst of heaven, having the everlasting gospel to preach to those who dwell on the earth—to every nation, tribe, tongue, and people—saying with a loud voice, "Fear God and* **give glory to Him***, for the hour of His* **judgment has come***: and worship Him who made heaven and earth, the sea and springs of water."*
*—Revelation 14:2, 3, 6, 7, NKJV, emphasis added.*

This new song is sung on Mt. Zion, but is deliberately inserted here between the universal command to worship the image to the beast (Revelation 13) and the announcement of the judgment in the first angel's command to "give glory to Him" (the Creator), the purpose of all true celebration worship.

This is the essence of the Minneapolis message. God's goodness and righteousness revealed by the judgment and freely offered by Christ, the Creator, require that we give Him glory and praise.[35] This is the essence of Minneapolis. True celebration worship must replace a law-and-behavior focus that makes us "as dry as the hills of Gilboa."

This is the essence of Waggoner's message, the only way to truly magnify the law. Only as we uplift the One who embodies the law, can He motivate true obedience. To give Him glory we must receive and proclaim His good news. His gift of righteousness is both the basis of judgment and the occasion for celebration!

## A "New Song" to Give Glory to God

The "new song" characterizing true celebration worship denotes a new experience of freedom from Babylon's authority and is based upon a new understanding of the good news of the judgment. In the three angels' messages, as amplified by the Laodicean message, Christ certifies removal of guilt, guarantees cleansing, and assures security in the testing time prior to His coming! The sole basis of this is a faith that comes from Christ and returns to Christ.

---

35  Other correlations include: (a) the proclamation of the universal message to all nations and peoples; and (b) the heavenly sanctuary as His place of judgment, implicit in Rev. 14:7. The only real difference is a tense change that intensifies the present urgency. The Revelator announces "the hour of His judgment *is* [already] *come*" (Rev. 14:7).

This assurance in judgment is the basis for rejoicing. Thus, true celebration worship must focus solely upon Him. Revelation provides the principle of true celebration worship in declaring:

*And they overcame him by the blood of the Lamb and by the word of their testimony, and they loved not their lives unto death. —Revelation 12:11.*

Our testimony is not to our victory but to "the blood of the Lamb," which provides victory. This is the essence of true celebration worship. We now consider the at-one-ment principle that must guide all true judgment hour celebration worship.[36]

---

36   While I was initially writing this chapter, my June 1990 issue of *Ministry* arrived with an editorial by David Newman and Kenneth Wade: "Is it Safe to Celebrate?" In their report of three Adventist celebration churches, they pose several vital questions to consider in evaluating this new-to-Adventists phenomenon. Some of these follow:

*"What constitutes a 'successful' church service? A successful church? successful pastor? Is there danger that some who view increased attendance and attraction of backsliders as success will begin to tailor not only their style of church service but also the message they proclaim to be popular and attractive in preference to truthful and honest? ...*

*"If success is defined in numbers, will we soon see increased competition between Adventist congregations to see who can put on the most exciting worship service? Does the celebration-type service magnify God or man? Does it bring commitment and a longing for the soon coming of our Saviour?*

*"Only time will answer our many questions. At the moment we caution against the two extreme reactions. Some are condemning what is happening without ever attending a celebration service or making any attempt to understand what the pastors are trying to accomplish. Others see celebration as the panacea for worship doldrums and are ready to jump on any 'success' bandwagon. The stakes in the battle for men's souls are far too high for us to judge without careful thought and reflection. Our only safety is found in prayer at the foot of the cross."*

# —Chapter 22—
# At-one-ment Celebration

*"Blow the trumpet in Zion. Consecrate a fast, Call a solemn assembly; Gather the people, Sanctify the congregation, ... Let the priests, who minister to the* Lord, *weep between the porch and the altar; Let them say, 'Spare Your people, O* Lord, *And do not give Your heritage to reproach, that the nations [Babylon] should rule over them. Why should they say among the peoples, "Where is their God?"'*

*"Then the* Lord *will be zealous for His land, and pity His people. The* Lord *will answer and say to His people, 'Behold, I will send you grain and new wine and oil, and you shall be satisfied with them; I will no longer make you a reproach among the nations ...'*

*"Fear not, O land; Be glad and rejoice, for the* Lord *has done marvelous things! ... Be glad then, you children of Zion, and rejoice in the Lord your God, for He has given you the former rain faithfully, And He will cause the rain to come down for you—the former rain, and the latter rain in the first month.*

*"You shall eat in plenty and be satisfied, and praise the name of the* Lord *your God, who has dealt wondrously with you; ... And it shall come to pass afterward that I will pour out My Spirit on all flesh; your sons and your daughters shall prophesy. ... And it shall come to pass that whoever calls on the name of the* Lord *Shall be saved. For in Mount Zion and in Jerusalem there shall be deliverance, ... Among the remnant whom the* Lord *calls." —Joel 2:15, 17–19, 21, 23, 26, 28, 32, NKJV.*

This passage, partially fulfilled at Pentecost (Acts 2:16–21), is ultimately to be fulfilled in the Day of Atonement heart-searching that must prepare us for the Latter Rain. Note how closely mourning and rejoicing are related. Strange as it may seem, the call to mourn for sin is a call to rejoice, for the mourner for sin is assured comfort (Matt. 5:4).

Failure to repent deprives us of radiant joy. Too often we are like the rich young ruler who "went away sorrowful" because he failed to repent of his covetousness (Matt. 19:22). Thus, we are unprepared for true celebration worship; and our lack of spontaneous praise to God in our services causes many to hunger for this experience, leaving them vulnerable to a false, manipulated celebration unrelated to deep, heart-felt repentance.

The judgment calls for repentance, and repentance provides occasion for joyful celebration worship. Thus, in the call of the faithful and True Witness to repent we need to hear His call for celebration worship. But, celebration worship is valid only as we respond to Laodicea's call for mourning our unbelief and pride. The last thing we need is to celebrate in masks that hide Laodicean self-satisfaction and that thus prevent mourning over sins and sinfulness.

## The Judgment Hour Feasts

Three judgment hour feasts telescope in Joel's Day of Atonement call to blow the trumpet to assemble the congregation in humility before the Lord. Trumpets, atonement, and the joyous harvest feast unite to transform the great judgment day from mourning to great joy. Thus, the first angel proclaims "the everlasting gospel," the glad news of Christ's judgment plan to give us true rest and rejoicing from the burden of sin and guilt.

The command to weep because of sins that misrepresent the character of God and bring us under the power of a world culture which influences our attitudes and/or lifestyles is a summons to heed the Laodicean message. And that message, as proclaimed at Minneapolis, delineates our problem and provides its cure.

The call is for reform in every area of departure from God's plan for our lives. This would certainly begin with conscious sin. But its primary thrust is to sin's roots which we but dimly see—pride, selfishness, and independence. Ignorance of the control these have over our lives blinds us to our own need for the 'straight testimony' call to Day of Atonement repentance, and judgmental attitudes toward others, even while imposing chronic guilt upon ourselves. In failing to grasp and apply the message of the 'straight testimony' to Laodicea by which Christ designs to free us, we in opposite ways unwittingly bury, or hide our guilt.

True celebration worship, however, requires neither our perfection nor full understanding of the message of the True Witness. It begins with our faith-acceptance of His testimony, in mourning over sin thus far exposed, to which we have been blind. God never has us face our guilt except to take it from us. The Spirit's first work is to confront us with sin. But He does so only to hasten our trip to the cross to receive His righteousness in exchange for our sin and guilt. He assures us that Christ, to whom we respond as we give Him our guilt and receive His righteousness, will stand in our place in the judgment:

> "And when He [the Spirit of truth] has come, He will convict the world of sin, and of righteousness, and of judgment." —John 16:8, NKJV.

Full comprehension of our Laodicean malady comes only gradually as we continue to respond. But joyful celebration is to mark our daily faith-acceptance of His righteousness, in a justification based on God's promise, not upon our obedience!

Thus, joyful celebration need not await any level of growth, but is released through faith-acceptance of Christ's rebuke as we claim His righteousness and His promise to write His law in our minds and hearts, thus enabling us to live victorious lives.

## Two Reasons to Celebrate: Substitute and Surety

The judgment provides two reasons for joyful celebration. First, it assures that, by faith, Christ becomes our *Substitute*. All who are "in Him" by faith are judged "in Him" by His perfection. Second, the judgment declares that He is our *Surety*. As Surety He assures that, "He which hath begun a good work in [us] will perform it unto that day" of final judgment and emancipation (Phil. 1:6). What could be greater cause for joyful celebration worship than to know Him as both our Substitute and our Surety (Phil. 3:8–11).

As we thus rejoice in justifying faith that is "without works," Christ displays His righteousness in and through us before the "heathen" who presently triumph over us because we lack the discernment and overcoming power of Christ's presence. Faith in Him as the source of all our righteousness, both internal and external, releases well springs of joy in spontaneous expressions of celebration over present acceptance and assurance of His victory. Any other celebration is shallow, superficial, and reveals resistance—if not open rebellion—to the Laodicean message.

## True Celebration Worship Results from Repentance

This kind of celebration needs no artificial stimulation. There is no music or artificially aroused emotion that can produce present freedom and assurance that He is not only the Author but the Finisher of our faith. And, when not restrained by a false sense of dignity, this assurance so deeply impacts our emotions as to call forth our highest praise to Him. This will impact our singing, so that even old songs will be sung with new enthusiasm and power.

Celebration that does not take sin and the True Witness seriously would parallel Israel's golden calf celebration and their declaration concerning this powerless idol, "This is your god O Israel that brought you up out of the land of Israel." It reflects Aaron's declaration, "Tomorrow is a feast to the Lord" (Ex. 32:4, 5, NKJV)! And it would imitate Israel's insistence on going up to conquer Canaan when unbelief and rebellion had resulted in God's command to turn back into the wilderness. Any celebration based on self-stimulated emotion involves sad deception.

We cannot produce the Spirit. We can only receive Him in obedient response to His loving rebuke by opening our hearts to Him and inviting His victory-producing fellowship.

The purpose of the Laodicean message is *at-one-ment*. Only in removing our self-justifying confidence can He draw us into His presence. And only consequent fellowship will permit completion of the heavenly atonement— "I will come in and sup with him" (Rev. 3:19–21). This key alone can release the well springs of lasting joy:

*"Purge me with hyssop, and I shall be clean; Wash me, and I shall be whiter than snow. Make me to hear joy and gladness that the bones which You have broken may rejoice." —Psalm 51:7, 8, NKJV.*

*"You will show me the path of life. In Your presence is fullness of joy; At Your right hand are pleasures forever more." —Psalm 16:11, NKJV.*

## Laodicean Self-Assurance: A Cover Up of Guilt

Sadly, a chronic Laodicean condition of pride and self-righteousness now prevents such celebration. Self-assurance is but a covering of guilt in vain attempts to engineer our own justification while resisting His sin-exposing, guilt-removing presence.[37]

Chronic, hidden guilt leads in opposite directions: (a) Conservatives seek to produce a sense of assurance by efforts to obey; (b) Liberals seek to alleviate guilt and produce joy by worldly entertainment, a false concept of justification, and by efforts to stimulate the feeling of God's presence. The first leaves insecurity which we unwittingly try to allay by judging Liberals; the second minimizes the importance of obedience, and seeks a justification by presumption.

Either way, consequent depression, resulting from chronic but often unrecognized guilt, blocks joy and either precludes celebration worship or intensifies the drive to artificially induce the Spirit and thus stimulate celebration worship. But neither a judgmental spirit nor worldliness can permanently satisfy. Both leave us empty and without true fulfillment.

Always at risk, we forever sense the need to reassure our security, either by works or by hyping ourselves in efforts to produce a "feeling" of His presence and acceptance.

---

37   While we must not stimulate our emotions and attribute this to the Spirit, we must also avoid repressing the joy of the Lord as we respond to the Spirit. It is proper to say, *Amen!* and to praise the Lord—even with feeling—to exclaim, *Hallelujah!* Laodiceanism robs us of spontaneity by depriving us of joy. Moreover, its atmosphere of self-satisfaction represses spontaneous expressions of joy in Him.

## False Security: Substitute for Joy-Releasing Faith

Dialectic patterns that focus on one side of truth or the other reveal attempts to attain security without being at-one with Him. Such false security is but a substitute for joy-releasing faith. We do greatly need genuine celebration worship! But it is imperative that we avoid dangerous short cuts by seeking to engineer emotional experiences that only appear to be the Spirit's moving. For, stimulating such emotional experience only confirms self-will and its contrived, false faith—a faith that thrives on feelings of security rather than in submitting to Him who is our Security because He is our righteousness—a righteousness claimed only by faith and never by feeling. Indeed, faith comes as the Spirit and truth unite in our hearts.

Appeal to emotion that bypasses reason is the badge of false religion. Emotions are vital and play an important part in worship, as in all other aspects of life. But when worship involves an attempt to arouse our emotions, our worship is of self rather than of the Creator. We, rather than the Creator, become the focal point of worship. We must ever guard against subordinating to emotion the Word by which He speaks to us, and thus His very presence. Nonetheless, music does have an important part in true worship in which we celebrate our joy in Christ Our Righteousness.

But it is only in response to that Word by which we are born again that we experience the joy-releasing justification which is the subject of our praise. Thus, we must avoid any approach to worship that tends to make preaching of the Word and its good news secondary to music or any other feature of worship, important as these may be.

# —Chapter 23—
# Collapse of Babylon's Dialectic Languages

*"Write to the angel of the church in Laodicea and say, Here is the message of the Amen, the faithful, the true witness, the ultimate source of God's creation. I know all about you: ... You say to yourself, 'I am rich, I have made a fortune, and have everything I want,' never realizing that you are wretchedly and pitiably poor, and blind and naked too." —Revelation 3:14–17, JB.*

Before rebuking Laodicea, His beloved remnant and "apple of His eye," for pride and unwitting self-deception, Christ introduces Himself in four authoritative terms. He, (a) "the Amen" and (b) "ultimate source of God's creation," challenges human reason to bow to the authority of His absolute truth, as (c) our "true Witness," and (d) His faithfulness in telling us the truth about ourselves. Moreover, before He diagnoses our problem as unwitting self-satisfaction and thus self-righteousness, He first assures us that He knows "all about" us.

The Laodicean rebuke for self-exaltation parallels the first angel's call to worship the Creator. By it the True Witness calls us to accept His authority as Creator and thus escape our unwitting self-righteous creature worship. Only thus can we heed the third angel's warning against the soon-to-come universal decree to worship the Papal Beast or his Protestant image.

That message points out the only way we will be able to resist the command to worship the beast or his image. Only as we first overcome the unwitting creature worship of self-righteousness can we triumph over the demand for creature worship by the universal confederacy now being formed.

This issue of worship always relates to authority. Both powers claim authority and both demand worship. Moreover, both have their signs of worship. Against the Creator's eternal Sabbath sign of true worship, Sunday, a sign of creature worship, is soon to be universally imposed. The issue underlying authority and worship is loyalty or disloyalty. To enforce loyalty to herself, the Papal beast not only seeks to enforce Sunday but to impose disloyalty to the Creator and His Sabbath sign. The mark of the beast doesn't need to be in the forehead, signifying belief; it can merely be in the hand, a symbol of surrender to the beast without really believing!

By contrast, Christ's seal or mark cannot be merely in the hand. It must be in a mind (Rev. 7:1–4; 14:1–7) that directs the hand in willing submission to His authority. *Not only what we believe, but also how we think, is involved.* That is why Laodicea's straight testimony is so important. For it has to do with the mind and hidden motives and warns us that mere external obedience not motivated by

His Spirit is actually disloyal worship of the creature. Loyalty to the Creator will be marked by a faith in Him that places reason and will under the authority of His Word.

## Fellowship with Christ Depends on Receiving the Straight Testimony

Christ's declaration of love and invitation to fellowship immediately follow His call to repentance. Such fellowship is conditional upon repentance and surrender of mind and heart in response to His loving straight testimony.[38] To ignore the authority of His discipline is thus to deny His fellowship and, however unwittingly, to repudiate our sonship (Heb. 12:6–8).

To receive the proffered gold ("faith that works by love," Gal. 5:6) we must honor the testimony of the True Witness concerning our self-deception. His justifying white raiment is available only to those who accept His indictment of self-justification and claim His righteousness by faith. Moreover, the eye salve essential to see truth correctly—especially truth concerning ourselves—is received only in surrender to the Spirit and to the Word by which He instructs us.

To discuss Minneapolis and justification by faith while ignoring Christ's Laodicean assessment can only mask self-justification. Whatever our theology, unless we heed His straight testimony that was resisted at Minneapolis and humble our hearts before God and before one another, we perpetuate the self-deception and worship of the creature against which He warns.

Fortunately, Christ looks in compassion upon our confusion. He knows that our problem has always haunted His people. But His purpose for us goes beyond that realized by any previous generation. Only in response to His straight testimony can we prepare for the 'loud cry' and defy the beast's authority, thus escaping the plagues prepared for him and all false worshippers. The reality of justification hinges not upon theological insight but upon response to the straight testimony of the Laodicean message resisted at Minneapolis.[39] *Not what we know but the way we think determines our destiny.*

---

38 "The True Witness says, 'Behold, I stand at the door, and knock.' Rev. 3:20. Every warning, reproof, and entreaty in the word of God or through His messengers is a knock at the door of the heart. It is the voice of Jesus asking for entrance. With every knock unheeded, the disposition to open becomes weaker. The impressions of the Holy Spirit, if disregarded today, will not be as strong tomorrow. The heart becomes less impressible … Our condemnation in the judgment will not result from the fact that we have been in error, but from the fact that we have neglected heaven-sent opportunities for learning what is truth" (DA 489, 490).

39 Tragically, our conservative/liberal polemics blatantly justify ourselves. Conservatives and Liberals alike demonstrate pride of spiritual understanding by mutual disdain

## Laodicean Call for Divine-Human Unity

To truly grasp the nature of our Laodicean disease requires a union of our human minds with the divine. This involves submission to the Spirit's direction and commitment to paradoxical thinking. (Technical understanding of 'paradox' is not essential, but uniting the poles of the truth is.) Without that union, which the Minneapolis message was designed to effect, we each tend to focus on part-truth, thus obscuring the call for death to self.

A shroud of darkness is necessary to preserve our false assurance, which Christ seeks to expose. To remove that shroud, He warns that, while we see ourselves as rich in theological truth and spiritual goods, we are actually destitute of spiritual graces. The key to proclaiming the invisible fall of Babylon in 'loud cry' power is found only in heeding the Laodicean message. Me must receive His riches, His robe of righteousness, and His spiritual eyesalve offered by His Spirit.

We cannot effectively draw people out of institutional Babylon while in a Laodicean state of unconscious servitude. Though completely separated from institutional Babylon, of which the beast and false prophet who promotes him are two of three segments, Laodiceans remain in some degree bound by her authority over self. Unless we take Christ's prescription we can never escape. And unless we escape, we are doomed to die in her dialectical chains.

for one another, not sensing that we must all answer to the one who patiently pleads, "Let me in" and "buy of me." Justification is not merely a doctrine. It is a gift from Jesus which we can receive only as we respond to the straight testimony to Laodicea by recognizing our own spiritual poverty.

# —Chapter 24—
# The Shaking of Adventism

*"You say, 'I am rich; I have acquired wealth and do not need a thing.' But you do not realize that you are wretched, pitiful, poor, blind and naked. I counsel you to buy from me gold refined in the fire, so you can become rich; and white clothes to wear, so you can cover your shameful nakedness; and salve to put on your eyes, so you can see. Those whom I love I rebuke and discipline. So be earnest, and repent. Here I am! I stand at the door and knock. If anyone hears my voice and opens the door, I will go in and eat with him, and he with me." —Revelation 3:17–20, NIV.*

This straight testimony of the True Witness to Laodicea addresses neither heresy nor apostasy. Christ's sole concern relates to a more subtle issue, the underlying cause of all these problems. His reproof of our self-righteousness must yet shake Adventism to its foundation by exposing the unconscious self-deception of our dialectical languages that continue to permit both of our cultures to remain blind to the fact that we are "poor, blind, and naked." Concerning this message that must either shake us up or shake us out, Ellen White declared:

*I asked the meaning of the shaking I had seen and was shown that it would be caused by the straight testimony ... of the True Witness to the Laodiceans. This will have its effect upon the heart of the receiver, and will lead him to ... pour forth the straight truth. Some will ... rise up against it, and this is what will cause a shaking among God's people. —Early Writings, p. 270.*

## Shaken Up, but not Shaken Out

Thus, the 'straight testimony' will either so shake us up as to have its desired effect, or it will shake us out—Conservatives and Liberals alike. When that testimony is permitted to remove fully the authority of self, it will at last have such an "effect upon the heart of the receiver" as to remove part-truth languages that have long held us in conflict. As we internalize its saving principles, we permit Him to seal our minds with His truth and love. This enables us to "pour forth the *straight* truth" in balance and power. That we might be thus shaken up but not out, God puts the final crisis on hold:

*Then I saw another angel ascend from the rising of the sun, with the seal of the living God, and he cried with a loud voice to the four angels to whom it was granted to harm the earth ... saying, "Do not harm the earth ... till we have sealed the servants of our God on their foreheads." —Revelation 7:2, 3, RSV.*

Christ Himself, the One from the east (literally "rising sun"), even now continues to hold back the final crisis as He waits for us to permit Him to imprint upon our minds "the seal of the living God" and send us forth with 'loud cry' power. But He can place His seal upon our foreheads (i.e., our minds) only as we assimilate whole truth as it is in Him. When we share truth in its purity and balance, while focusing on Him, every entity in the worldwide religio-political society (i.e., Babylon) will be shaken and God's other "sheep" will be released from their bondage.

*"After this I saw another angel coming down from heaven, having great authority; and the earth was made bright with his splendor. And he called out with a mighty voice, 'Fallen, fallen is Babylon the great ...' Then I heard another voice from heaven saying, 'Come out of her, my people, lest you take part in her sins, lest you share in her plagues'" —Revelation 18:1-4, RSV.*

## Only by Coming into Christ Our Righteousness Can We Fully Come out of Babylon

Paradoxically, the straight testimony that swells into the 'loud cry' of the Latter Rain has two sides; without both there is no power. To come out of something soon to be eternally destroyed is vain unless we come into something that will eternally save—Christ our Righteousness.

The 'loud cry' began to sound in 1888, but its notes were immediately so muffled by opposition and consequent confusion that we still cannot completely agree on what those notes were. That cry announces that corporate "Babylon is [morally] fallen" and calls God's people to "Come out of her." But, to call them out with power, we must first come out from her influence. Nor can anyone fully "come out," without coming into Christ and abiding in Him in whom we are to draw His people. Only those who come into Him can escape falling with Babylon.

Indeed, only "in Him" who declares, "I am the truth," can we learn to speak the balanced language of the whole truth that unifies rather than divides. Only by the language of whole truth can we give the 'loud cry.' To effectively call others out of Babylon, we must first develop a language of "straight" balanced truth and a culture of love which those who come out can safely come into. For Babylon's authority extends to some extent to all whose competing languages enforce her pride.

Thus, far more than the "letter of the law" is involved in calling God's people out of institutional Babylon. To leave an institution of Babylon and enter Adventism does not assure escape from Babylon. For by our dialectical languages cultural Adventists bow to her authority. This could make those coming out of institutional

Babylon even more vulnerable to her power, for they assume they have escaped when they are still in bondage.

## It Takes Time to Fully Escape Babylon's Part-Truth Languages

Membership in God's remnant church is no assurance of acceptable Creator worship. Nor does it guarantee becoming part of His true remnant. We may be members of His organization without being born into His spiritual kingdom. Indeed, even being born again does not assure escape from the influence of Babylon's 'split-truth' languages. It takes time and diligence to learn how to consistently speak the balanced language of heaven's "straight truth."

Thus, the 'loud cry' message that began to sound at Minneapolis (1SM 363) demands deeper insight into both the call to come out and the call to enter in. It must fully internalize the Minneapolis principle, permitting it to humble our glory "in the dust." The essence of that cry is Behold your Creator God; find your righteousness in Him, your High Priest. Only as we maintain our focus upon Him as our divine-human High Priest can we escape Babylon's authority in our lives and help other captives escape. Only in receiving Him as our sole righteousness does entering His earthly body, the church, offer safety.

This requires repudiation of the authority of Babylon's king-self and renunciation of the self-centered principle of his government which operates by means of its conflict-stimulating languages. And to do this we must behold Christ and commit ourselves to the painful task of learning to think paradoxically. We must habitually seek to grasp and hold in focus both sides of any and every revealed truth, regardless of our own present perspectives. Only then will we find a unity in fellowship that reflects unity in truth.

## Minneapolis Offers Not Something *from* Christ: It Offers *Christ Himself*

Minneapolis calls us to behold the lovely Jesus—Emmanuel, the God-Man who links us to His Father. In beholding Him, we become changed and respond to His motivation to renounce puppet-king self, through which the real king of Babylon, Satan, rules the world. This permits the Spirit to share with us both sides of righteousness—Christ as objective Substitute to cover our guilt; and Christ as our Surety, guaranteeing His presence to transform our lives and to assure a verdict of eternal justification in the judgment.[40]

---

40  *Theology in Crisis*, pp. 142–156. "Substitute and Surety," a favorite phrase for Ellen White, expresses the unity of the objective and subjective work of Christ for and in the soul.

Aside from this two-fold righteousness there is no righteousness at all. Assurance based on one element of truth that is not integrated with the other only exposes Laodicean confusion, resulting from infatuation with and enslavement to Babylon's puppet-king self.

The Minneapolis message calls us not to get something *from* Christ, either to cover guilt or to help us obey, but to *receive Him* as our righteousness (justification), whose presence empowers obedience. He takes our guilt and enables us to experience His righteousness.

Minneapolis thus unites the cross and the ministry of Christ, as does the apostle Paul, who repeatedly insists that hope in Christ's death (i.e., objective to us) is valid only in His resurrection to minister, a ministry we receive subjectively in the new birth and through life in the Spirit: "If Christ be not raised your faith is vain; ye are yet in your sins" (1 Cor. 15:1-4, 14–20)?

The risen Christ Himself both justifies and sanctifies. "In Christ," He is both "our righteousness [i.e., justification], and our sanctification" (1 Cor. 1:30). Having died for our sins, He was resurrected to both justify us by His blood and to sanctify us by His presence.

## Justification vs. Sanctification Conflict Advertises Ignorance of Minneapolis

Throughout the Old Testament types, *it is the priestly ministry of the blood— not the sacrifice per se—that makes the sanctuary atonement* (i.e., Lev. 5:6; 6:6, 7). Satan's strategy is to get some to focus upon justification and enter into conflict with others who defend sanctification. In so doing, each diminishes his own part-truth by belittling the other![41]

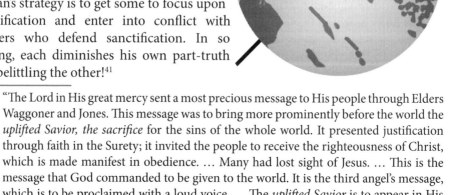

41 "The Lord in His great mercy sent a most precious message to His people through Elders Waggoner and Jones. This message was to bring more prominently before the world the *uplifted Savior, the sacrifice* for the sins of the whole world. It presented justification through faith in the Surety; it invited the people to receive the righteousness of Christ, which is made manifest in obedience. ... Many had lost sight of Jesus. ... This is the message that God commanded to be given to the world. It is the third angel's message, which is to be proclaimed with a loud voice, ... The *uplifted Savior* is to appear in His *efficacious work as the Lamb slain, sitting upon the throne,* to dispense the priceless covenant blessings. ...

"This is the testimony that must go throughout the length and breadth of the world. *It represents the law and the gospel, binding up the two in a perfect whole."* —TM 91, 92, 94, emphasis added.

We are saved by neither justification nor sanctification! Nor even by both together! We are saved, rather, by a living, loving Savior. Having given His life as a substitutional sacrifice for our sins, He now gives Himself with the merits of His sacrifice as Surety that "in Him" we are certain to pass the scrutiny of the judgment! Thus, to receive Him is to receive Him as Substitute and our Surety.

Our battle over the relative importance of justification versus sanctification advertises our ignorance of Minneapolis principles that unite both the poles of truth in Christ and are to unite all believers in truth as it is *in Him*. Both Conservatives and Liberals have learned to use Minneapolis terminology; but this often masks the absence of its spirit and principles.[42]

When we focus on law and grace in the light of Him who is Truth, we see not two different commodities to be secured from Him, justification and sanctification, but two aspects of what it means to receive Him. Neither alone is valid. For neither can be received alone. We receive both by receiving Him. And, in Him, they blend into a single essence.[43]

## Preparation for the Divine-Human Wedding

To truly grasp the inner unity of the third angel's message and of its Minneapolis expression, we must give close attention to the issue of worship. True worship, in contrast to false worship, always relates to intimate unity between the worshipping creature and the Creator, characterized by humble submission to the Creator. There are numerous *forms* of worship, but only two *kinds*—worship of the Creator and worship of the creature. Creature worship, no matter what objects or philosophies are involved, always involves worship of king-self, the medium through which we ultimately worship the false god Lucifer, who is the Devil and Satan.

It is from this false worship that the Creator died to set us free. Thus, the good news is that, in the final judgment, our Judge and Advocate intends to forever break the final link to false worship and free us forever to worship and give glory to Him:

---

42  A primary difference between pre–1888 and post–1888: before 1888 we developed our conservative dialectical language of law in reaction to the evangelical language of grace imposed by enemies outside the church; now liberal forces within lead the evangelical attack. As a result, Conservatives intensify their **dialectical** focus, but now largely aim their defensive guns upon Liberals within.

43  "Genuine faith appropriates the righteousness of Christ, and the sinner is made an overcomer with Christ; for he is made a partaker of the divine nature, and thus divinity and humanity are combined" (1SM 464).

*"Fear God and give glory to him; for the hour of his judgment is come: and worship him that made heaven, and earth, and the sea, and the fountains of water." —Revelation 14:7.*

We are not merely free to worship Him, we are forever united with Him in marriage bonds that make us eternally one with Him:

*"And I heard as it were the voice of a great multitude ... saying, Alleluia: for the Lord God omnipotent reigneth. Let us be glad and rejoice, and give honor to Him: for the marriage of the Lamb is come, and His wife hath made herself ready. And to her was granted that she should be arrayed in fine linen, clean and white: for the fine linen is the righteousness of saints. And he saith unto me, Write, Blessed are they which are called unto the marriage supper of the Lamb. And He saith unto me, These are the true sayings of God."*
*—Revelation 19:6–9, JB.*

This wedding celebrates an eternal, intimate union between Christ and His people to which He has long looked forward, but that can be realized only as we heed His Laodicean rebuke—His love appeal to his bride. Our fickleness in flirting with the enemy has long delayed the longed for consummation of His union with His bride. Indeed, the Laodicean message is a call to the marriage, a marriage that only awaits our response in receiving the wedding garment He offers, His own righteous character. By grateful response to that message we enter an intimate fellowship with Him that self has too long resisted.

## The Divine-Human Union Must Now Be Formed

It is *now* that this divine-human unity is to be formed. A wedding does not unite a couple. It sanctifies, makes legal, and celebrates an intimate union already formed but not yet consummated. Only in responding to Christ's reproof and allowing Him to enter and fellowship with us can we know the sinless culture of his righteousness and learn to speak a fully balanced language of "straight truth" by which we are to call all His "other sheep" out of Babylon. This alone will prepare us for consummation of the long delayed and greatly anticipated marriage!

# —Chapter 25—
## Liberation from Babylon

*"After these things I saw another angel coming down from heaven, having great authority, and the earth was illuminated with His glory. And He cried mightily with a loud voice, saying, Babylon the great is fallen, is fallen ..."*
—Revelation 18:1, 2.

The first angel's judgment announcement, which many fear and consider bad news, is declared "the everlasting gospel," or "the eternal good news"! And the third angel bears the good news that a triumphant and obedient people will, with undeviating faith in Jesus, triumph over Satan's greatest deceptions and be ready for His coming in the clouds of heaven.

But, what about the second angel's message? It has a lot of bad press. Some consider it arrogant to announce the fall of Christian churches. Is the fall of Babylon good news?

To answer that question we need to consider the history of Israel's captivity and the fall of ancient Babylon which released them from that captivity. God's prediction of the fall of Babylon was surely good news to the Jews and that release is a prophetic type of the fall of Babylon in our day!

Yet, is it not arrogant to identify the Protestant churches as well as the Papacy as parts of modern Babylon? Especially when we ourselves are divided by Babylon's 'split-truth' languages?

The answer is both yes and no. Unless we understand Babylon and our own captivity to her languages, the answer is, *Yes!* It is arrogant! But when we grasp the nature of Babylon and our relation to her, the answer is, *No!* We then identify with all others who must escape.

Only as we truly face Christ's 'straight testimony' will we begin to grasp how that message applies to ourselves. And only as we fully escape Babylon's languages can we grasp what it means to "come out of her." Then only can we proclaim this great good news to the world with such power that the system of Babylon collapses and sets God's honest people free.

When truly proclaimed, the second angel's message is not an indictment of others. It is a confession of our universal need for deliverance from self, the source of her power. It involves a joyful testimony that Christ is able to deliver His people from satanic power.

Otherwise, we have difficulty answering the charge of arrogance in calling ourselves the remnant and identifying all others with Babylon. Only by responding to the Laodicean-Minneapolis message can we escape the charge of arrogance. And that will require deliverance from our endless conflicts that testify to our own bondage, not *in* Babylon, but *to* Babylon. To answer the charge of arrogance we must do so in light of the ancient type.

## Sin Causes Bondage; But God Permits Bondage to Save His People

*"Thus the slain shall fall in the land of the Chaldeans, ... For Israel hath not been forsaken, nor Judah of His God, ... though their land was filled with sin against the Holy One of Israel. Flee out of the midst of Babylon, and deliver every man his soul; . . for this is the time of the LORD's vengeance ..."* —Jeremiah 51:4–6.

The literal fall of any man or nation is always preceded by a moral fall. Thus it was with Judah, who had been in spiritual bondage for centuries. Because of Judah's "sin against the Holy One of Israel," He at last sold them into captivity to Babylon, who held them for decades. God, nevertheless, remained faithful to His people. Indeed, He permitted their national bondage only to prepare them to become "free indeed" (John 8:32).

At the very time He sent Judah into captivity, God, through Jeremiah, predicted their release after seventy years (Jer. 25:11). The God who could no longer protect His people and, because of their rebellion, gave them over into the hand of Babylon, did not forsake them.

Their captivity provided unusual opportunities for Babylon's leaders to become acquainted with the living God. Yet, despite the revelation of Himself to Nebuchadnezzar through His faithful witnesses, later kings disregarded the Creator. As a result of her own moral fall, Babylon would become too weak even to defend herself. Prediction of her fall to the Medes and Persians was good news to God's people, to whom He had long before named Cyrus as Babylon's conqueror—even describing how he would take the city (Isa. 44:26–45:1).[44]

---

44 The entire book of Isaiah is a type, portraying the conflict between Christ and Satan. Northern Israel's bondage to Assyria blends into Judah's bondage to Babylon, but the focus is upon Christmas Deliverer of His end-time people in eternal defeat of Satan, king of mystical Babylon. Israel's corruption and consequent bondage to Assyria and Babylon are types of our present bondage to mystical Babylon. The good news is that Revelation prophetically uses this overthrow of Babylon, in miraculous deliverance of God's people to portray Christ's ultimate destruction of Satan's antitypical Babylon. Both Isaiah and Revelation end with the destruction of Christ's enemies and God Himself coming to dwell with us in the New Jerusalem (Isa. 11–14, 21, 41–48, 65, 66; Rev. 12–22).

## Righteous Man from the East, King of the
## North, to Conquer Mystical Babylon

A century and a half before Jeremiah's birth, Isaiah had predicted Babylon's fall. But more important than Cyrus' victory over literal Babylon is the assurance that He will deliver his remnant people from bondage of more than a century and a half. For He raised up Cyrus, not merely to conquer Babylon, but to provide a prophetic type of Christ's deliverance of His remnant people from the great system of mystical Babylon, not *in* which but *to* which many of us as yet remain bound.

Pointing beyond the type to God's antitypical judgment, Isaiah predicts the raising up of "the righteous man from the *east*" and declares concerning Him, "I have raised up one from the *north*, and He shall come from *the rising sun* [east]" (Isa. 41:2; 42:25). But, why north and east?

Babylon's king entered Judah to conquer and capture Jerusalem from the east of Jerusalem, descending from the north. Cyrus, type of the true King of the north, would overthrow typical Babylon to free His people to return to Jerusalem, the type of Christ's New Jerusalem capital, by also coming from the east and descending from the north.[45]

By this type we are informed of two "kings of the north": a *false*, usurping king who captures and holds God's people in bondage; and a *true*, liberating King, who sets His people free.[46] While Isaiah, Jeremiah, and Ezekiel portray this by typical prophecies relating to Jerusalem and ancient Babylon, Daniel, in symbolic but non-typical prophecy, applies Cyrus' function directly to Christ, the true King of the north, soon to deliver spiritual Israel from mystical Babylon's control.

## Tidings from the East and from the North …
## Babylon Comes to His End

Significantly, Daniel also portrays Papal Babylon's exploits against "the holy covenant … even to the time of the end" as activities of the usurping "king of the north" (see Dan. 11:13–16, 28–43). But just as modern Babylon reaches the height of her power and glory, she falls helplessly before Christ, the divine deliverer. Note Daniel's antitypical echo of Isaiah's type:

---

45   In several prophets, "north" is a symbol of both the usurping king of Babylon and Christ, the true King of the north (e.g. Eze. 26:7). Jeremiah begins with a prophecy of Babylon identified as "out of the north" (Jer. 1:13-15). Ezekiel begins with a portrayal of Christ "out of the north" (Eze. 1:4). Isaiah identifies both old Jerusalem and Babylon with the "north."

46   Isaiah, Jeremiah, and Ezekiel present typical prophecies through Babylon and Israel, but point antitypically to the conflict of Satan vs. Christ and spiritual Israel. Daniel's prophecies point symbolically but directly to Christ's victory over the Papacy.

*"But tidings from the east [literally "the rising sun"] and from the north shall alarm him, and he shall go forth with great fury to exterminate and utterly destroy many ... ; yet he shall come to his end, with none to help him. At that time shall arise Michael, the great Prince who has charge of your people."*
*—Daniel 11:44–12:1, RSV.*

It is impossible for even those of us who have escaped institutional Babylon to free ourselves from her dominating influence as imposed by her split-languages of law and grace. That is why we must depend upon Christ, the antitypical Cyrus to set us free. We need to understand that Satan, supreme king of Babylon, is only able to deceive through part-truth. He has no power over God's people except deception. And this requires that he make part-truth appear to be the whole, while causing others to treat the balancing part-truth as the whole. And with each set against the other in resistance to the other's balancing principle, neither can discover whole truth. Thus, Satan makes sport of us by stimulating our constant pitting of part-truth against part-truth.

In the first indication of true and false kings of the north, Isaiah portrays Lucifer's attempt to displace Christ in heaven and take His throne (typified by the table of "showbread," or "bread of the presence" on the sides of the north in the ancient sanctuary):

*"How you have fallen from heaven, O star of the morning, son of the dawn! ... You who have weakened the nations! But you said in your heart, ... 'I will raise my throne above the stars of God, and I will sit on the mount of assembly in the recesses of the north. ... I will make myself like the Most High.' Nevertheless you will be thrust down to Sheol, to the recesses of the pit."*
*—Isaiah 14:12–15, NASB.*

Lucifer appears to succeed in his attempt to usurp Christ's place "in the recesses," or "sides of the north." Indeed, through Babylon, he, to a large extent, controls us by manipulating our part-truth languages. The good news is that Babylon is about to collapse and her king "shall come to his end and none shall help him."

Not only do Isaiah, Jeremiah, and Daniel portray Babylon's king as reigning over the kings of the earth and exalting himself to the very height before collapsing (see also Eze. 28:14–17), so also does John in Revelation. In each case, just as he appears to succeed, Christ brings him to an end. John unites all the Old Testament prophecies together as he portrays the final collapse of Satan's three-fold Babylon (i.e., pagan spiritualism, the Papacy, and apostate Protestantism; Rev. 16:12–19).

## Michael Soon to Stand up to Overthrow Babylon

Michael, the antitypical Cyrus, is soon to arise and free His people. As He does, Babylon, led by the false king of the north, will be helpless to hold them.

But Michael will not overthrow Babylon until we allow Him, as did Cyrus, to use us as His servants in accomplishing this. This means that we must repudiate the dialectical languages by which Babylon imposes conflict upon us. We must acquire a balanced and pure theological and spiritual speech and a pure culture that will unite us and permit Him to reveal Himself through us.

Only by the revelation of His righteousness through His people (in contrast to the self-righteousness He deplores) can Babylon's authority and power be overthrown. And that can only happen through a dynamic union between Christ and His people in which He is seen in all the glory of that love which drove Him to the cross and now causes Him to patiently await the consummation of our spiritual marriage with Him.

## True Understanding of the Second Angel's Message Precludes Arrogance

Such unity with our Creator and with each other in love results in the worship in spirit and in truth for which He calls. And this is what will precipitate the collapse of Babylon's power. Yet this calls for death to self. When self is dead, Babylon is powerless to enforce her authority.

The straight testimony of the faithful and True Witness to Laodicea is a declaration that Babylon's authority over us has not yet fallen. Our self-satisfaction in having escaped institutional Babylon has left us in bondage to her self-righteousness, and thus judgmental attitudes.

Until we, individually and corporately, grasp and apply the straight testimony to Laodicea we cannot truly understand the second angel's message. Such attempts to proclaim it to the world appear arrogant, for we continue to deny that reality even as we seek to proclaim it.

That is why Christ sent His special message at Minneapolis. It was designed to humble our glory "in the dust" so that He can reveal the glory of His self-sacrificing character in and through us. This revelation will collapse Babylon and destroy her glory. But that can never happen until we honor the Creator's straight testimony by acknowledging our own self-righteousness and dying to self. Only as we submit our human reason to His Word can Babylon's power over Laodicean minds be broken.

Then only can we give the 'loud cry'—Babylon is fallen! That cry and its power will so alarm the king of Babylon that every agency will be set in motion either to control or to destroy God's people. This will climax in the death decree to all who refuse to worship the creature (Rev. 13:8–18). But to no avail, for all who choose to behold Christ as Creator-God and High Priest, claiming Him as Substitute and Surety, will then be free to come out of her!

## Babylon's Fury Unleashed by Its Inability to Enforce Its Languages

As we respond to the glory of the Sun of Righteousness, He will arise upon us and the glory of His character will be revealed through us. He will free us to repudiate the authority of that puppet king-self, who alone can authorize Babylon to impose 'split-truth' languages upon us.[47] As we thus permit Him to free us from all creature worship, the third angel's message will swell to the 'loud cry' of Revelation 18:4, releasing multitudes of Babylon's captives.

Whom we worship is determined by what king we serve. And whom we serve is determined by our focus, whether upon Christ or upon self. Christ longs to remove our unwitting idolatry and arise upon us as His denominated people. He is eager to seal His character in our minds, forever preventing any defection to Babylon's king Satan.

As we are freed from his authority over us we will proclaim His message in 'loud cry' power, calling those who remain in institutional Babylon to come out before the plagues fall.

Enraged at his inability to enforce conflict-imposing languages upon us, the false king of the north "shall go forth with great fury to destroy … utterly" by a universal death decree. "Yet, he shall come to his end and none shall help him." For "at that time Michael," the true king of the north, shall stand up to deliver His people (Dan. 11:44–12:1; Rev. 14:6–12; 13:12–17).

## Babylon's Wrath Not Stirred While We Speak Its Languages

Thus, the collapse of Babylon's power over God's people precipitates the final conflict between Christ, the true King and Satan, who usurped control of God's people. His 'split-truth' languages will at last forever lose their power to deceive true believers in Christ.

But, we have as yet hardly ruffled Babylon's king. When fully aroused, the dragon-serpent of Eden will exhibit his rage as never before (Rev. 12:7–9, 17). At present he has little to fear. As long as we are divided by his dialectical languages, he knows we will remain feeble. Indeed, as long as he can divide and control us without our knowledge or suspicion, he will be careful not to arouse us to recognize the urgency of responding to Christ's insistent plea.

Neither Conservatives nor Liberals now reveal a power sufficient to shatter Babylon's pride and self-complacency. Only by "looking to Jesus" and receiving His presence, which alone brings both poles of truth together, will we be able to give

---

47 "Arise, Shine; for your light has come! And the glory of the Lord is risen upon you. For behold , darkness shall cover the earth, and deep darkness the people; but the Lord shall arise over you, and His glory will be seen upon you" (Isa. 60:1, 2, NKJV).

the Babylon-shattering 'loud cry.' Our only hope is to respond to Michael's 'straight testimony' and depend on His Spirit to help us apply the whole truth. As we keep our focus upon the "Author and Finisher of our faith" (Heb. 12:2), our worship will be of the Creator alone.

As we are set free from Babylon's control by submitting self to the exclusive rule of Jesus our Substitute and Surety, Babylon will lose her authority over us! Christ is vastly more powerful than Satan, but His principles in restoring our freedom require our consent as He empowers our will.

When we, as victorious witnesses, unitedly proclaim a message that exposes Babylon's conflicting languages, she will lose her control, not only over us but over honest souls we call out, who are now also unwittingly bound by Babylon's 'split-truth' languages. Then only will we truly develop the culture of heaven and prepare to call others to join in the culture of God's love:

*The last rays of merciful light, the last message of mercy to be given to the world, is a revelation of His character of love. The children of God are to manifest His glory. In their own life and character they are to reveal what the grace of God has done for them. —Christ's Object Lessons, pp. 415–416.*

As honest-hearted people witness our unity and purity of speech, they will then understand what it means to come out of Babylon and reject the authority she exercises by her part-truth languages. Until then, those whom we draw out of institutional Babylon remain to a significant degree subject to her authority. But as we focus upon Christ and lead them to do the same, He will empower them to refuse the command to worship the beast and his image—even at the risk of martyrdom. Babylon's only power over us and them at that time will be over bodies that are surrendered to Christ as temples of the Holy Spirit.

*"If you abide in My Word, you are My disciples indeed. And you shall know the truth, and the truth shall make you free." —John 8:31, 32, NKJV.*

# —Chapter 26—
# Summary and Conclusions

In this book our focus has been the two basic cultures of Adventism with their corresponding languages that are in continuous conflict with one another. A conservative culture with its language focused sharply upon law fails to adequately place the law within the context of grace; whereas a liberal culture focused on grace fails to place grace in the context of God's law.

By no means do I imply that every Adventist is imbalanced or that there is uniformity in the two basic language groups. There are many subcultures and degrees of balance and/or imbalance. Nor have I intended to judge individuals or groups, but merely to deal with a corporate problem which we face, along with all humanity. Until we better understand that problem, we will be unable to share in the final victory between Christ and Satan and unable to give the loud cry, "Babylon is fallen, is fallen," in a manner to release its captives.

God lovingly and sympathetically seeks to expose our weaknesses, but not criticize us. It is, rather, to free us from our guilt and bondage that He exposes a problem we must understand before we can go free. The principles apply to all; but different degrees of language control are exercised over us; and there are many degrees of growth and victory.

It is urgent that we not judge one another. It is appropriate to recognize and seek to understand both cultures; yet it is not well to think of one another in terms of culture. Indeed, to the ultra Conservative, virtually everyone is a Liberal. To the ultra Liberal, nearly every one is a Conservative. Instead of judging one another, let us each understand the other better and we will see one another more sympathetically. For, whatever our culture and whether extreme or moderate, we all have the same spiritual disease, pride and self-righteousness.

We all know and often remind others that we should not judge. But one of our most serious "sins" is to judge those we identify as judgmental. Not only does that put us in the judgment seat, but they may be growing and daily gaining victories which we cannot see.

To clarify our conflict of languages, I have used the terms Conservative and Liberal. The purpose, however, has not been to judge, but to demonstrate that, though we defend opposite principles, we have a common problem of imbalance. It is thus important that we not think of each other in terms of Liberal or Conservative, but see in each other struggling children of God with common underlying needs and weaknesses, recognizing that we are all prone to imbalanced emphases in our various approaches to truth. Only as we respond to divine counsel to "press together, press together, press together" (2SM 374) can we help balance each other.

The greatest test of our love for God is our love for each other. And Christ's greatest longing is that we receive His love and share it with one another. Jesus says to us, "By this shall all men know that you are my disciples, if ye have love one to another" (John 13:35). His "Day of Atonement" prayer, just before His crucifixion, must yet be fulfilled:

> "That they may be one; as thou, Father art in me, and I in thee, that they also may be one, even as we are one: I in them, and thou in me, that they may be made perfect in one: and that the world may believe that thou hast sent me." —John 17:21.

*Whole* commitment to *the whole* truth can alone make us one with Christ. And only in oneness with Him can we find unity with each other. For this evidence the world has been waiting. And this is the heart of God's message of "straight truth" that is to transform us.

Efforts to become like Him in character can only make us legalistic unless we daily behold Him whom to behold is to know and to know is to love. Since His love is omni-directional, to truly love Him is to share that love unstintingly with all His children, whatever their attitudes toward us. This is the only path to perfection. A love relationship with Him that is shared with others will alone give us confidence to face the judgment.

> "Love has been perfected in us in this: that we may have boldness in the day of judgment; ... There is no fear in love, but perfect love casts out fear, because fear involves torment. But he who fears has not been made perfect in love. We love Him because He first loved us." —1 John 4:17–19, NKJV.

Indeed, unselfish love will make us seek to understand and harmonize with each other and avoid trying to prove the other wrong. Pride is the real author of our conflicts, not differences of concept. And pride is the central nerve of Babylon and Satan, her king. This does not, however, suggest that uncompromised truth is unimportant. We can seek to understand others and still show the greatest respect for purity of "straight truth." We must recognize that the Lord may want to use the other to help us see some aspect of truth of which we are not aware—even if the other is in some way in error.

Love for truth matched by love for those with whom we differ will bring us together to seek the Spirit to open our minds to the whole truth. The "straight truth" will free us from Babylon and enable us to help others go free. Let us with all our hearts seek to escape her authority by entering into personal relationship with Jesus and absorbing His love that we may share it selflessly with all, especially with the erring, who can never recover except by receiving that love.

It takes time to learn a new language. Let us now earnestly study and practice the language of heaven—the language of love—and press together as we seek to grasp the full range of truth which alone can keep us from imbalance and error.

# —Appendix A—
# Paradoxical vs. Dialectical

Words are often used in many different and sometimes even in opposite ways. As a result, many conflicts are primarily a matter of semantics. That is, they involve arguments resulting from different uses of words. This, unfortunately, is even true of the terms 'paradoxical' and 'dialectical.'

Hastings' *Encyclopaedia of Religion and Ethics* defines **'paradox'** as allowing for either *real* and *only apparent* contradictions, but concludes by affirming that the essential nature of truth is its having two apparently contradictory elements: "*Truth* may be—perhaps even in the end *must be—paradoxical*" (vol. ix, p. 632, emphasis added). This confirms the basic meaning of paradoxical as dipolar truth with converse principles that only seem to contradict each other; though, in reality, each is essential ("must be") to the other, for the integrity of each depends upon its proper relation to the other. In other words, it shouldn't be a matter of "either … or," when it's "both."

The *Literary Dictionary*[48] defines **'dialectic'** as:

1. The art of formal reasoning, especially the procedure of seeking truth through debate or discussion;

2. The reasoning or logical structure that holds together a continuous argument or exposition;

3. The interplay of contradictory principles or opposed forces, as understood in the European tradition of philosophy influenced by G. W. F. Hegel and including Marx and Engels. Some schematic versions of *dialectical* philosophy speak of a unification of opposites in which the *thesis* is opposed by the *antithesis* but united with it in a higher *synthesis*.

These definitions illustrate, but do not exhaust, the different uses of these terms. My use, however, is specific and relates only to that used by Plato and Hegel, as presented in definition 3. Plato pit democracy against his own oligarchical system to make first one system and then the other appear superior. In the end, however, he makes it clear that the only rational solution is for the system of oligarchical government to overcome the system of democracy, so that the ruler rules, the warrior wars, the worker works, and the slave slaves, and that no one in any caste be permitted to break out of their ordained caste and move to another.

---

48  Found at <http://www.answers.com/dialectic>.

# —Appendix B—
# Ellen's Use of the Theological Ellipse
## by Herbert E. Douglass*

P hilosophers and Theologians have been discussing the perennial objective-subjective dichotomy for at least 2500 years, sometimes with verbal hand grenades. We see the sharpest distinctions in this dichotomy early on when we listen to Plato, on one hand, and Aristotle, on the other. Some call it the difference between Theology A and Theology B. Or Pole A and Pole B. Or Kierkegaard's Religiousness A and Religiousness B.

With the risk (1) of being too superficial and (2) for the purpose of this limited study, I will define Pole A as the study of "God's mighty acts" (G. Ernest Wright) and Pole B, as the "rational effort to explain what is" (Durwood Foster), and (3) I will propose that Ellen White is the "theological construction engineer" who demonstrated "a balanced affirmation" of the age-old tension within the dichotomy. Using common terms we can list the dichotomy as follows:

### The Objective/Subjective Dichotomy

| FORMAL Pole A: | FORMAL Pole B: |
|---|---|
| Objective | Subjective |
| God | Man |
| Authority | Responsibility |
| Answers | Questions |
| What things mean | What things are |
| Concreteness, particularity | Abstract |
| Personal experience | Rationality, demonstrable |
| Requires personal decision/response | Universally accessible |
| Supernatural | Natural |

The challenge for all truth-seekers is to transcend this Objective-Subjective Dichotomy; if Adventists do not, we are lost in academic verbiage and mutually exclusive presuppositions, like everyone else. Our challenge is simply to recognize that truth is not either "objective" or "subjective." How is this done?

1.  This question led to an epiphany in my doctoral program. Day after day, in seminars with Buddhists, Catholics, Mennonites, Presbyterians, Congregationalists, Methodists—you name it—all I heard was learned

* Condensed from Adventist Theological Society lecture, Nov. 22, 2008.

opinions, debated back and forth, with learned teachers adding to the bifurcations. It dawned on me that truth had to transcend the prevailing differences of opinion, which to me were not all wrong. I found myself saying, "You are both right." And that became a new journey in understanding this Grand Canyon between Pole A and Pole B.

2.  Soon I saw that there is no truth in the "either/or" copout. Nor is there a "middle way" that so many contemporaries cling to and call themselves "centrists." No "mean" between "two errors!" The more one stresses Pole A, that much more Pole B objects and the war continues between good men and women, stuck in their mutually repelling attempts to state Truth.

    For me, only a correct understanding of New Testament faith transcends the "impossible possibility." But note, I emphasize New Testament faith, because the word, *faith*, has probably been the most divisive word in Christian history, and never more so than today.

3.  And that is when my daily reading of Ellen White opened the door that helped me to understand such thinkers as Emil Brunner over against Barth and Bultmann (who between them became Pole A and Pole B). Ellen opened my door to New Testament faith, not the Catholic faith, not the Lutheran glaube ["faith" in old high German], not the Pietist faith, nor the New Spirituality (emerging church) faith. And that fresh insight opened up the door wider to the meaning of the Atonement, Commandment-keeping, grace, justification, etc. Everything was now connected to everything else and the Plan of Salvation no longer had *non sequiturs* for me. I suddenly understood the Great Controversy theme.

---

And so my three questions that are only three suggestions:

1.  How does Ellen White with her insightful theological discussions sort out this subjective-objective dichotomy that has literally divided all theological and philosophical thinking for thousands of years, to this day?

    She saw biblical truth in the form of the ellipse with two foci or focuses: Pole A and Pole B. She saw the value of each focus even as a football recognizes the value of both foci, or Poles. *Truth is not a circle but an ellipse with two foci.*

    I have illustrated this biblical ellipse with one question: When you want a glass of water, do you ask for a glass of hydrogen, or should you ask for a glass of oxygen? We say that is a silly question. If you want water, you expect $H_2O$. For water, we can't have one without the other. It is the truth of the ellipse.

    Biblical truth is not a game played between two circles, two contrary theologians, each one aiming to lead to truth—anymore than oxygen or hydrogen will lead to water. Truth does not lead to a standoff that many

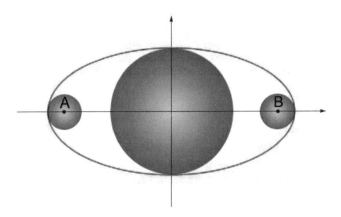

**An ellipse as compared to circles.** An ellipse is not a single circle with just one focus, or two separate circles with separate foci. It is a single geometric shape with a double foci.

theologians call a 'paradox.'[49] The paradox is a human construct and melts in the light of the ellipse.

2. How did Ellen steer the fledgling Adventist movement through the theological/philosophical mine fields in the nineteenth century, without whom we would exist today as only a footnote in the pages of American history?

One of the best examples of her theological savvy occurred in her contribution to what could have been a colossal quagmire in 1888–1900. Prior to the 1888 General Conference, Adventist leaders were valiant objectivists.

Faith was more a matter of believing, rules trumped transformation. Objectivists feared the loss of theological purity at the expense of the faith experience championed by Methodists, antinomians, *et al.* But Ellen brought New Testament common sense by transcending the objectivism/subjectivism dichotomy.

Not an easy time for a truth-bearer: Ellen described her involvement in the 1888 crisis: "The hardest and most incomprehensible tug of war we have ever had among our people" (3SM 177.4).

*Note how Ellen transcended both sides*: "The Lord in His great mercy sent a most precious message to His people through Elders Waggoner and Jones. This message was to bring more prominently before the world the uplifted Saviour, the sacrifice for the sins of the whole world. It presented *justification through*

---

49   Douglass' use of 'paradox' here illustrates the confusion of opposite uses of 'paradox' and 'dialectic.' By 'paradox' he means what I call 'dialectic,' which splits the principles of truth and pits one principle against the other.

*faith in the Surety*; it invited the people *to receive the righteousness of Christ, which is made manifest in obedience to all the commandments of God.* Many had lost sight of Jesus. They needed to have their eyes directed to His divine person, His merits, and His changeless love for the human family. ... I have no smooth message to bear to those who have been so long as false guideposts, pointing the wrong way. If you reject Christ's delegated messengers, you reject Christ. Neglect this great salvation, kept before you for years, despise this glorious offer of *justification through the blood of Christ* and *sanctification through the cleansing power of the Holy Spirit,* and there remaineth no more sacrifice for sins, but a certain fearful looking for of judgment and fiery indignation" (TM, pp. 91, 92, 97).

3. How can Ellen in the 21$^{st}$ century help Adventists avoid the oscillation between the subjective-objective tensions that have generally divided all other Christian churches to this day?

Let's look at a few examples of how keen, thorough, and consistent Ellen is as she employs the ellipse of truth to inform her theological teachings:

A. ○ Ellipse #1: Saviour and all-powerful Mediator. "The arch-deceiver hates the great truths that bring to view an *atoning sacrifice and an all-powerful mediator.* He knows that with him everything depends on his diverting minds from Jesus and His truth. Those who would share the benefits of the Saviour's mediation should permit nothing to interfere with their duty to perfect holiness in the fear of God" (GC 488).

B. ○ Ellipse #3: Redeemer and Intercessor. "*The intercession of Christ in man's behalf in the sanctuary above is as essential to the plan of salvation as was His death upon the cross.* By His death He began that work which after His resurrection He ascended to complete in heaven. ... Through defects in the character, Satan works to gain control of the whole mind, and he knows that if these defects are cherished, he will succeed. Therefore he is constantly seeking to deceive the followers of Christ with his fatal sophistry that it is impossible for them to overcome. But Jesus pleads in their behalf His wounded hands, His bruised body; and He declares to all who would follow Him: 'My grace is sufficient for thee.' 2 Corinthians 12:9 ... Let none, then, regard their defects as incurable. God will give faith and grace to overcome them" (GC 489).

Purchased and Kept. "Everyone who will break from the slavery and service of Satan, and will stand under the blood-stained banner of Prince Immanuel will be kept by Christ's intercessions. Christ, as our Mediator, at the right hand of the Father, ever keeps us in view, *for it is as necessary that He* should keep us by His intercessions as that He should redeem us with His blood. If He lets go His hold of us for one moment, Satan stands ready to destroy. Those purchased by His blood, He now keeps by His intercession" (MS 73, 1893, quoted in *Seventh-day Adventist Bible Commentary*, vol. 6, p. 1078, par. 5).

C.  ⬭ Ellipse #4: Sacrifice of Jesus and Holy Spirit. *"The Spirit was to be given as a regenerating agent, and without this the sacrifice of Christ would have been of no avail. …* Sin could be resisted and overcome only through the mighty agency of the Third Person of the Godhead, who would come with no modified energy, but in the fullness of divine power. It is the Spirit that makes effectual what has been wrought out by the world's Redeemer. It is by the Spirit that the heart is made pure. Through the Spirit the believer becomes a partaker of the divine nature. Christ has given His Spirit as a divine power to overcome all hereditary and cultivated tendencies to evil, and to impress His own character upon His church" (DA 671).

D.  ⬭ Ellipse #5: Righteousness by Faith—Imputed and Imparted. "Our only ground of hope is in the righteousness of Christ imputed to us, and in that wrought by His Spirit working in and through us" (*Steps to Christ*, p. 63).

"The only way in which he [Jesus] could set and keep men right was to make himself visible and familiar to their eyes. … The whole purpose of his own mission on earth—to set men right through the revelation of God. . . . When the object of his mission was attained—the revelation of God to the world—the Son of God announced that his work was accomplished, and that the character of the Father was made manifest to men" (ST Jan 20, 1890).

E.  ⬭ Ellipse #6: God's part and man's in the salvation process. "God works and cooperates with the gifts He has imparted to man, and man, by being a partaker of the divine nature and doing the work of Christ, may be an overcomer and win eternal life. The Lord does not propose to do the work He has given man powers to do. Man's part must be done. He must be a laborer together with God, yoking up with Christ, learning His meekness, His lowliness. God is the all-controlling power. He bestows the gifts; man receives them and acts with the power of the grace of Christ as a living agent. … *Divine power and the human agency combined will be a complete success, for Christ's righteousness accomplishes everything*" (FW 26, 27, emphasis added).

F.  ⬭ Ellipse #7: Faith and works. "Abraham's faith was made manifest by his works. 'Was not Abraham our father justified by works, when he had offered Isaac his son upon the altar? Seest thou how faith wrought with his works, and by works was faith made perfect?' James 2:21, 22. There are many who fail to understand the *relation of faith and works.* They say, 'Only believe in Christ, and you are safe. You have nothing to do with keeping the law.' But genuine faith will be manifest in obedience" (PP 153, 154).

G. Many more such as: repentance and faith, forgiveness and cleanse, etc.

How to make this practical in our work today?

In typical religious language, Conservatives form the "objectivist" circle and Liberals are in the "subjectivist" circle, although these labels are far from satisfactory. Each circle is emphasizing something correct, timely, and needed. Even as water is not formed until the circles of hydrogen and oxygen are reformed as an ellipse, so the partial truths represented by Conservatives and Liberals do not set forth the full picture of truth until they are both cast within the ellipse of truth.

Key words for Conservatives (for which they will fight to the death) are: transcendence, authority, orthodoxy, rootage, law, structure, security, and grace—*all good words to hold on to.* But the historic weakness of Conservatives is often a misunderstanding of the character of the transcendent God. They often emphasize authority at the expense of human responsibility and freedom. ...

Key words for Liberals (for which they also will fight to the death) are immanence, freedom, responsibility, reason, flexibility, meaning, relevance, and personal faith—*also good words to hold on to.* The historic weakness of liberalism is rooted in its subjectivity. ...

In post-modern times, both Conservatives and Liberals cross lines when they no longer ask, "Is it true?" But rather, "Does it work?" Pragmatic experientialism puts the question, "What is there in it for me?" rather than the more Biblical "What am I going to do about it?"

Ellen White puts these questions into proper perspective as she appeals to both the traditional Conservatives and Liberals to see the answers within the Great Controversy Theme. She understood well this historic standoff between these two circles and how, within Adventism especially, both Conservatives and Liberals alike will fail to see the whole picture—if they fail to see the ellipse of truth that transcends the weaknesses of both Conservatives and Liberals.

She wrote: "The progress of reform depends upon a clear recognition of fundamental truth. While on the one hand, danger lurks in a narrow philosophy and a hard, cold orthodoxy, on the other hand there is a great danger in a careless liberalism. The foundation of all enduring reform is the law of God. We are to present in clear, distinct lines the need of obeying this law" (MH 129).

Conclusion: "Hard, cold orthodoxy," and "careless liberalism" are the end results of placing truth in two circles rather than letting truth be truth in its elliptical form. Ellen transcends these two circles by uniting authority with responsibility, doctrinal security with heart assurance, so that the Seventh-day Adventist Church does not need to fall back into the theological arguments and constructs that divide all other churches. The purpose of God's Plan of Salvation is fulfilled when former rebels become willing, loyal sons and daughters of God—so set in their mind and heart that they will never be moved to ever say *No* to God again. Ever! They are the perfect product of a self-communicating God and a habitually responsible man or woman.

Ellen's theology is the surest route to avoid the quicksand of objectivism and subjectivism.

# Creation or Evolution—The New Evidence
## by Gary J. Warner*

There *is* new evidence and it is rolling in like a tsunami! As I reviewed Dr. Moore's manuscript for *Adventist Cultures in Conflict*, I was struck by his perception and depth of understanding of what is happening within Adventism in the area of creation and evolution. He exposits a clear understanding of reality: the issue is cultural, subjective and presuppositional. I thought I was alone among Adventists, with rare exception, speaking out in public against the tide of confusion about creation and evolution.

It was the early sixties and the space race was on! I was reading everything I could get my hands on about space and the implications of man in space for the future of society. With Khrushchev rattling his nuclear missiles and the prospect of the world blowing itself up, it occurred to me that our only hope was to get off! Get into space; go to Mars; colonize the solar system—quick! Oh for the enthusiasm of youth! Responding to a radio appeal by President Kennedy, I decided to move forward to a career in aerospace engineering. I have had the great satisfaction of contributing to the Apollo Manned Lunar Landing program in 1969, the original Viking Mars Lander program in 1976, several interplanetary space exploration programs, and the design of several earth-orbiting spacecraft.

For the last ten years I have been attending conferences all over America, reading widely and speaking on the creation-evolution issue. There has been a virtual absence of Adventists in the public arena proclaiming Christ as Creator based on His own claims and the laws of nature itself. Dr. Walter Veith of South Africa is a notable exception.

As with the health message to some extent, it seems that the Lord has searched to find willing and obedient servants to give the first angel's message with clarity

---

* Gary Warner writes as an applied scientist/engineer and as a former non-Adventist evolutionist. He earned engineering degrees at Penn State University and the University of Arizona and completed graduate courses in Astronautics and Aeronautics at the University of Washington. He interned with Northrop Space Laboratories on military space systems and with NASA in Houston on the Apollo Manned Lunar Landing Program. For 15 years he was employed with The Boeing Company and for 21 years with the Hewlett-Packard Company. For 25 years Mr. Warner was a licensed Professional Engineer in the State of Washington. He is currently Director of Research and Development with The Wonder Company. He is a lifetime member of Tau Beta Pi engineering society and has held membership in numerous technical and professional organizations. He holds seven U.S. patents.

during our lifetime. Evidently His search has led to those willing to "hear" and "see" and "go," though they are "still to be found in their communion" (Sunday keepers). Nonetheless, the first angel's message IS going out in our lifetime and with increasing speed and power, but not much from Adventist tongues or pens—except now, I see Dr. Moore's.

The Adventist conference discussed in chapter 13 reminded me of a trait I have observed in many Adventists, more often than not those highly educated. For eight years (1999-2007), I taught "Creation or Evolution–The New Evidence" Sabbath School class at the Auburn, California Adventist church. During that period, about 100 local members attended for varying lengths of time. Apparently due to the uniqueness of the theme, a number of people visiting from around the USA and a few from other countries were attracted as well. The trait involves trusting what scientists in specific fields conclude (fallible, human reasoning) as objective, "scientific" truth. In reality such Adventists, like many other Christians, apparently assume or believe that their most admired "scientists" in their favorite fields of study have reached valid, objective, "scientific" conclusions. Unfortunately, this trust based on assumption is considered good enough, with no thought of checking the "scientific" conclusions in terms of known laws of nature.

In fact, evolutionary "conclusions" are evolutionary suppositions worded as conclusions, enhanced with a lot of scientific jargon. Sadly, I saw pride and prejudice that excluded any sense of the laws of physics, mathematics and information science which rule out molecules-to-man evolution. It seemed that people who presumed to be "scientifically" astute were somehow obligated then to make sure they didn't disagree with the experts who claim to have "proven" evolution.

Of course, they wouldn't have to do all the research themselves, but only avail themselves of much excellent work already being done in several technical fields by highly qualified scientists with a biblical worldview at institutions such as the Institute for Creation Research, Answers in Genesis and others. The vast majority of reputable scientists doing objective work, with results supporting Intelligent Design and creation, are non-Adventists. And a number of them are former evolutionists! A broad set of solid scientific resources supporting the creation account of history is increasingly accessible by visiting their websites. Not the least of these works is a computerized analysis corroborating Moses' use of Hebrew language in Genesis supporting a literal 24-hour day, six-day creation.

Why do many Adventists choose to trust the conclusions of their favored "scientific" sources? A likely answer to this question became apparent to me during those teaching years (1999–2007): fear of embarrassment, or worse—rejection, academically, professionally, socially and personally (self-worth). Of course for a rare few, this fear is justified by potential loss of grant money and even salary, depending on their particular employment situation. But there also appears to be a rationalized fear by potential loss of "face" or acceptance in academic, professional, social and even religious communities where popular consensus is highly valued to self-worth.

But objective reality existing in the laws of nature strips away the cloak of subjectivity in popular "science" consensus, revealing another reality, in a word—pride, in three words—lack of humility. In essence, man's subjective, fallible imaginings are chosen as Authority over the truth specifically revealed by the Creator in His Word. And that choice is made against much support for the reality of intelligent design generally revealed in nature by the Creator.

There is a rare but excellent Adventist kick-off point to grasp the truth about what is real, objective science and what is only speculative, subjective "science" philosophy. I heartily recommend <www.ScienceAgainstEvolution.org> as one starting point.

Here is a *high-level summary* of some things I've learned in my search for truth.

1. Origins can neither be proven or duplicated. No one has ever observed how things came into existence from nothing, whether elemental or living. All scientists view the same evidence, the same facts, but interpret them according to the framework of their preconceived worldview.

2. Each person's chosen position or belief on origins depends on what is valued as the most reasonable sources of support. For example, man can analyze, deduce and verify many things observable in nature. But man as a finite creature has ideas about origins that are constantly changing because, many times, speculations don't hold up to the laws of nature and reason. On the other hand, *if* an infinite and all-knowing Creator *revealed* how we got here, we would expect those ideas to prove reliable.

3. We are saturated with reports of support for evolution from a multitude of sources on a regular basis. This continual input typically excludes what appears to be obvious to many observant and objective people—intelligent design throughout nature. This has caused me to think more and more carefully about the actual reality of things we are being told.

4. *There is reasonable support for the Bible's account of history* from the laws of nature in various fields of knowledge. For example, the law of cause and effect (a cause must at least have all the characteristics of the effect it produces, such as in the case of intelligence, feeling, emotion, love, beauty, morality and will—all must come from a cause with such conscious personality). Other reasonable support can be found in astronomy (such as non-isotropy in the universe, young comets, moon's recession, earth's magnetism, etc.), in geology (predictions expected from a global flood, helium recently found in deep earth rocks, Po-14 radiohalos, etc.). And there is good support from archaeology and history.

5. I have read statements by leading evolutionists in different fields who admit that random chance processes cannot have produced the complexity and fine tuning of life as we know it. They further admit there is *no known mechanism to cause evolution*. They also admit that it appears that the universe and life are designed for a purpose. *The argument* by the world's greatest evolutionary minds, the leaders of molecules-to-man evolution philosophy is that God did not create anything, but **something** "natural" *must have* evolved everything. *Anything*, but a Creator! *Anything*, but *the* Creator!

6. Molecules-to-man evolution is *a belief that actually defies several known laws of nature*, for example: the first and second laws of thermodynamics, the law of biogenesis, the laws of information science, genetics and probability, the law of cause and effect and the existence of consciousness, intelligence and conscience. It is becoming increasingly clear to me that molecules-to-man evolution is a religion masquerading as "science." And I am also beginning to see that "natural selection" wears the mask of an evolutionary god.

7. Of interest for Christians at large, increasingly today, technically qualified intellectuals in many fields of knowledge are exposing a *host of assumptions and speculations* in the molecules-to-man evolution model. Just a few of these are: Spetner, Kenyon, Behe, Gentry, Dembski, Johnson, Hunter, Austin, Baumgartner, Gitt, Humphreys, Silvestru and White. There are many, many others.

Then considering the Adventist portion of the body of Christ, it is interesting to notice that Ellen White cautioned strongly about beliefs that contradict the Bible's plain teaching on the Lord Jesus Christ as our Creator and Savior. (These may be found in *Patriarchs and Prophets* and *The Great Controversy*.)

# The Testimony of an Adopted Son
## by Keith Stokes*

I first became acquainted with Dr. Moore in Bridgeport, CT in 1970. He was the new Pastor of the Brooklawn Seventh-day Adventist Church in Bridgeport, Connecticut. I had recently graduated from Academy and was living at home while attending the University of Bridgeport.

Pastor Moore had a profound impact upon my life as a young man in my late teens and early twenties. He was more than a pastor to me, he was also a father and mentor. During the many hours I spent with him in his home and travelling together over a period of approximately four years, I learned some of the most important things in my life. In my relationship with him, I "downloaded" some important life skills such as integrity, moral purity, non-judgmentalism, and faithfulness to God and the Church. I was challenged by example to study the Word for myself and develop critical and independent thinking skills. There was a contagious spiritual energy about him, pouring out from deep within him, that I always admired. I could sense that his heart had been filled each morning from his personal time with the Lord.

Keith Stokes, M.A., M.Div.

I was not his only spiritual son. There was another young man who also followed closely in his footsteps. Robert Banks, now ministerial director of the Potomac Conference, was also mentored by Dr. Moore, and he became a life-long brother to me as well. Bob was a new convert at the time, and he and I would often find ourselves discussing spiritual insights inspired by Pastor Moore to challenge each other to think broadly and inclusively. In hindsight, Pastor Moore essentially adopted two sons.

I may not be able to remember the specifics of a sermon 40 years ago but the inspiration of the one preaching resonates within me to this day. Truth is not just

---

* Keith Stokes has had advanced instruction in brain science and recovery from emotional trauma in connection with the Life Model Development Team. Other education includes a Masters in Ed. in Math from the University of Bridgeport, CT in 1976 and a Masters in Divinity from Andrews University in 1994. His passion is equipping people with the understanding that can help them experience healing and maturity in the light of the Sanctuary. His "Understanding How the Brain Works in the Context of Relationships" Seminar is a life-changing series.

theoretical; it is also relational. Pastor Moore developed genuine relationships with all of his church members. He carried us on his heart.

Pastor Moore also set a baseline for me in expository Biblical study those Sabbath mornings that few have equaled in the 39 years since. At the time I could not articulate a framework or specific paradigm, but I could sense the underlying theme. No matter what the subject, I always sensed balance and a broad inclusive reasoning. I knew that Pastor Moore had a methodology and a central theme. Many a sermon would sound with a clarion call from Isaiah 60:1–2:

> *"Arise, shine; for thy light is come, and the glory of the* Lord *is risen upon thee.*
> *For, behold, the darkness shall cover the earth, and gross darkness the people:*
> *but the* Lord *shall arise upon thee, and his glory shall be seen upon thee."*

At the time I was majoring in mathematics at the University of Bridgeport and I probably would have expressed what I heard in terms of an ellipse with two centers [as has Herbert Douglass] as Pastor Moore came from at least two directions simultaneously. He would often begin with an apparent conflict of principles, and then a central theme would emerge out of the cloud. Pastor Moore would often stretch those two poles so that we could see truth more clearly but the orbit would always remain in delicate balance between those two poles. I would look forward with eager anticipation each Sabbath for a message and the Lord would tuck away many gems in my heart that I would keep for the rest of my life.

Even as I write, it occurs to me that, in my seminars on Brain Science Maturity and the Sanctuary, I have been unconsciously influenced by this principle of the two poles. It is actually the central principle of healthy brain function. Simply stated, mature and practical truths exist in the marriage of left hemisphere and right hemisphere processing. This can clearly be demonstrated starting in the Garden and enlarging to Revelation.

To this day he is still "Pastor" Moore to me because that best defines our relationship. The highest honor I can give him is that, as a pastor at heart, he remains a spiritual parental role model for me. I remain profoundly influenced by his example.

# —Index of Sources—

Answers in Genesis at <http://www. answersingenesis.org> [150]

Behe, Michael J. Darwin's Black Box: The Biochemical Challenge (New York: Simon and Schuster, 1996) 307 pp. [152]

Canright, D. M., Adventism Renounced: After an Experience of Twenty-eight Years (New York; Chicago: Fleming H. Revell Co., 1889), 413 pp. [4]

Dawkins, Richard. New Statesman, quoted in Richard Milton, Shattering the Myths of Darwinism (Rochester, VT: Park Street Press, 1997), pp. ix, x. [58]

Douglass, Herbert. Adventist Theological Society address, November 22, 2008. [21, 142–148]

———. Messenger of the Lord (Boise, ID: Pacific Press, 1998), pp. [9]

Giem, Paul. letter. [59]

Hasel, Frank M. "Thomas Kuhn's Concept of Paradigm and Paradigm Change," Journal of Adventist Theological Society, Vol. 2, Number 2, Autumn, 1991. [61]

Hastings, James. The Encyclopaedia of Religion and Ethics (Edinburgh: T&T Clark, 1994) 12 vols. [12, 141]

Johnson, Phillip E. Darwin on Trial (Downers Grove, IL: InterVarsity Press, 1991), 220 pp. [60]

Kuhn, Thomas. The Structure of Scientific Revolutions (Chicago: University of Chicago Press, 1962), 172 pp. [60]

The Literary Dictionary [141]

Milton, Richard. Shattering the Myths of Darwinism (Rochester, VT: Park Street Press, 1997), 272 pp. [57, 58]

Moore, A. Leroy. Adventism in Conflict (Hagerstown, Review & Herald Publ., 1995), 191 pp. [7, 8, 11, 72, 160]

———. Questions on Doctrine Revisited!: Keys to the Doctrine of Atonement and Experience of At-one-ment (Ithaca, MI: AB Publishing, 2005), 288 pp. [8, 160]

———. Theology in Crisis: or, Ellen G. White's concept of righteousness by faith as it relates to contemporary SDA issues (Corpus Christi, TX: Life Seminars, 1979, 1980). [8, 88, 125, 160]

Newman, David and Kenneth Wade: "Is it Safe to Celebrate?" Ministry, June 1990, pp. 26–29. [111]

Polak, Frederick W. The Image of the Future: Enlightening the Past, Orienting the Present, Forecasting the Future (Amsterdam; New York: Elsevier Scientific Pub. Co., 1973), trans. from Dutch, 2 vols., 319 pp. [31]

Popper, Karl R. The Open Society and Its Enemies, vol. 1, The spell of Plato; vol. 2, The high tide of prophecy: Hegel, Marx, and the aftermath (London: Routledge, 1945) [31–34]

Rice, Richard. "Believing, Behaving, Belonging—Exploring a Larger View of Faith," Spectrum, Vol. 20, No. 3, April 1990, pp. 22-31 at <http://spectrummagazine.org/files/archive/archive16-20/20-3rice.pdf>. [75–77, 82]

Seventh-day Adventist Bible Commentary, Francis D. Nichol, editor (Review and Herald Publ. Assn., Washington, D.C., 1956, 1980), vol. 6. [146]

Seventh-day Adventists Answer Questions on Doctrine: An Explanation of

Certain Major Aspects of Seventh-day Adventist Belief. Prepared by a Representative Group of Seventh-day Adventist Leaders, Bible Teachers, and Editors (Takoma Park, MD: Review and Herald Publ. Ass., 1957), 720 pp. [17, 19]

Spectrum, "A Bold Precarious Faith," Vol. 20, No. 3, April 1990. [75]

Times Online, Feb. 2, 2009 accessed Feb. 18, 2009 at http://www.timesonline.co.uk/tol/comment/faith/article5705331.ece [76]

"Upheaval in the East: Hidden Wealth; Disclosures of the Ceausescus' Riches Appall Many Threadbare Rumanians." The New York Times, Dec. 21, 2008. [38]

Veatch, Henry B. Two Logics: The Conflict Between Classical and Neo-analytic Philosophy (Evanston: Northwestern University Press, 1969), 280 pp. [25, 30, 31]

Warner, Gary J. "Creation or Evolution—The New Evidence" [149–152]

Webster's New Collegiate Dictionary (Springfield, MA: G. & C. Merriam Co., 1977), 1536 pp. [22]

White, Ellen G. Christ's Object Lessons (Washington, D.C.: Review and Herald Publ. Assn., 1900, 1941), 436 pp. [135]

———. The Desire of Ages [DA] (Mountain View, CA: Pacific Press Publ. Assn., 1898, 1940), 863 pp. [120, 146]

———. Early Writings of Ellen G. White (Washington, D.C.: Review and Herald Publ. Assn., 1882, 1945), 324 pp. [123]

———. The Great Controversy Between Christ and Satan [GC] (Mountain View, CA: Pacific Press Publ. Assn.,

1888, 1911), 722 pp., 718 pp. [51, 145, 147, 152]

———. The Ministry of Healing [MH] (Mountain View, CA: Pacific Press Publ. Assn., 1905, 1942), 540 pp. [148]

———. Patriarchs and Prophets (Washington, D.C.: Review and Herald Publ. Assn., 1890, 1958), 805 pp. [152]

———. Reflecting Christ (Hagerstown, MD: Review and Herald Publ. Ass., 1985), 382 pp. [79]

———. Selected Messages, book 1 [1SM] (Washington, DC, Hagerstown, MD: Review and Herald Publ. Assn., 1958), 448 pp. [125, 127]

———. Selected Messages, book 2 [2SM] (Washington, DC, Hagerstown, MD: Review and Herald Publ. Assn., 1958), 488 pp. [138]

———. Selected Messages, book 3 [3SM] (Washington, DC: Review and Herald Publ. Assn., 1980), 510 pp. [144]

———. "The Future," Advent Review & Sabbath Herald, Dec. 31, 1857 [23]

———. Steps to Christ (Battle Creek, MI: Review and Herald Publ. Co., 1892), 126 pp. [146]

———. Testimonies to Ministers and Gospel Workers [TM] (Boise, ID and Oshawa, Ontario, Canada: Pacific Press Publ. Assn., 1923, 1944, 1962), 566 pp. [65, 126, 145]

———. "God Made Manifest in Christ," The Signs of the Times, Jan. 20, 1890. [146]

"Zoo Cancels Ticket Deal with Creation Museum," Associated Press, Dec. 6, 2008. [39]

# —Scriptural Index—

# Other books by A. Leroy Moore

Order these from www.aleroymoore.com. Many additional books and other materials relating to these issues are available at www.BalancedFaith.org.

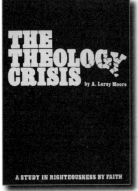

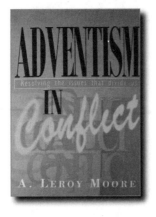

A 1979 examination of Dr. Desmond Ford's Theology of Legal Justification

Resolving the issues that divide us.
(Out of print—hope to republish soon.)

An examination of the entire *Questions on Doctrine* controversy in the context of reconciliation.

◆

# Books by Kevin Morgan

Order these from your local Adventist Book Center 1-800-765-6955

Is there something missing in your busy life? Historical evidence for God's special day of rest
(Special pricing for cases of 50)

A faith-building study of Inspiration and Ellen White's use of sources in *The Desire of Ages.*